A HEALER IN EVERY HOUSEHOLD

SIMPLE SOLUTIONS FOR STRESS

Dr. Manon Bolliger, ND

NATUROPATHIC MEDICAL DOCTOR

Author of the No.1 Bestseller
*What Patients Don't Say if Doctors Don't Ask:
The Mindful Doctor Patient Relationship*

D0775652

Author's Photo: Nancy Ackerman
Cover Design: Booklerk, Katarine Nskvsky

DISCLAIMER:
This book has been created to inform individuals with an interest in taking back control of their own health. It is not intended in any way to replace other professional health care or mental health advice, but to support it. Readers of this publication agree that neither Dr. Manon Bolliger, ND nor her publisher will be held responsible or liable for damages that may be alleged or resulting, directly, or indirectly, from their use of this publication. All external links are provided as a resource only and are not guaranteed to remain active for any length of time. Neither the publisher nor the author can be held accountable for the information provided by, or actions resulting from accessing these resources.

"I dedicate this book to my mother — who taught me that "where there is a will, there is a way" and to my father — who taught me how to 'celebrate life'; both gifts that have supported me in my journey and for which I am grateful."

Acknowledgements

I would like to start by acknowledging all my patients, my students, fellow practitioners, and the researchers that have inspired me to write this book.

I couldn't have hoped for wiser mentors in the world of publishing than Mary Weinzenbach, Brendon Bouchard and Julie Salisbury of the Vancouver Authors' Circle. Tracy Marcynzsyn who helped me with the original edits, Terry McGraw who knew how to turn the "mots justes" of my French-studded manuscript into silky English prose, and Michael McConkey who fine tuned this current edition.

Finally, my family's support has been invaluable in the writing of this book. This book could not have been written without the understanding and support of Leana and Janael, the enthusiasm of Sagan, the recommendations of Michael McConkey and the deeply supportive, calming inspiration of my partner, Tony Joyce.

A special thank you to Derek Rydell for helping me with naming *"A Healer in Every Houshold"*.

Table of Contents

Preface

Six years have passed since I wrote *What Patients Don't Say, when Doctors Don't Ask: The Mindful Doctor-Patient Relationship* and since then, nothing much has changed with the conventional medical paradigm. In fact, it has become clearer than ever that health itself is subject to the whims of technocrats. As a society, only time will tell, whether the choices that were made to avoid the death of our aging population warranted the death by suicide, abuse and neglect of the other sectors in the population. Only time will tell whether the proposed solutions to the 2020 pandemic crisis will serve to amplify the tenants of our deepest assumptions that we can control nature without regard to the health and wellbeing of our bodies. It has become increasingly important that the "patient," or "health consumer," realize that the best defense in health is prevention, working to support the body's immune system. Our Body is smarter than we think.

In the following chapters, you will understand the full context and framework underpinning the movement to engage the healer, in every household.

As many of us have experienced, relying on outside expertise can be very challenging. Scientific research has been used for political and financial agendas. The governing health Boards receive funding which creates the potential for conflicts of interest. Values people hold dear to their heart cause friction and judgement when expressed. People are angry, fearful, and are awakening to questions they would never have previously asked themselves. In the name of "public health," we have lost sight of the reality for families trying to balance work-life priorities during these challenging times. We have lost sight of the epidemic of loneliness, isolation and dependency.

We have brought to light the failings of our monetary system, the environmental implications of our industrial practices, the bankruptcy of our political systems and the systemic "moral" control over freedom to information. We have witnessed the power and control of pharmaceutical and philanthropic funding in support of medical schools, research, and "solutions" in health care. We have seen and felt the impact of the "no consequence, no liability, no responsibility" infrastructures we have endorsed. An infrastructure we thought was there to support us has instead profited from our acquiescence.

It is a rude awakening to any victim-minded individual that the solutions to move us forward will never come from the infrastructure that brought us here. The solution comes in the form of radical self-responsibility. But rest assured. Our Body is smarter than we think! Learning to work through the body to calm the mind is not only essential but extraordinarily effective.

It is my fervent hope that this book will inspire self-directed patients, who know that true health is a decision that each of us has the power and responsibility to make. I am also excited to participate in the movement for better health, with the numerous doctors who came to this career path to share their knowledge and expertise, creating a vibrant, healthy, and loving world.

Since revising my last book- What Patients don't Say If Doctors Don't Ask, I have also grown as a doctor and as a person. Although finding the right health care team is a true blessing, there is much that you can do to turn your health around. This book does not address what is amply available on the internet. I do not cover the foods one should or could eat or suggest a bunch of missing supplements. All this is important but most important is to develop a mindset for health. A deep understanding of how our current medical system operates and what you can do to go beyond your symptoms to embrace a whole new way of looking at your life.

After frequent patient requests, I created a simple protocol that can be followed in the comfort of your own home. This protocol amplifies your healing and prevents dis-ease. I have created "Reboot Your Body" for the patient. I have devoted a chapter to it in this book to encourage you to take immediate action. In my experience, working with the physical body is the most direct way of initiating the healing process.

You may not understand all the fancy medical terms, the diagnosis or how our physiology and nervous system work but healing itself is simple. What stops us from taking charge of our health is the belief that experts have answers we need before we can act. This is why so many people run in circles, from one specialist to the next, one body part assessment to another, test after test, only to finally recognize that we are whole Beings with an integrated system. Solutions for our parts rarely address the underlying issues. Before dis-ease, there is stress. If you understood how managing stress would fundamentally change your view on illness and equip you with a way to live your life, you would embrace the choices you make in life that sustain and maintain health. You would know that you are the healer. You are the healer in your household, your family and maybe even your community. There is a part of you that is yearning to shift, to learn something new. My goal is to ignite the passion in every person to take charge of their health, start the healing journey, and trust and love their own body.

Introduction

The playing out of the 2020 pandemic has revealed that we are at a crossroads in health – an actual paradigm shift. You get to choose how to make sense of what is happening. Either you believe that nature is evil and that you are helpless prey: a victim susceptible to attack who must hide to protect yourself. Meanwhile you must wait for the delivery of a solution from elsewhere: maybe a drug that will kill this " virus" or a vaccine that will render us "immune" to it on the premise that by activating a small part of our immune system with intradermal nano luminescent micro tatoo, our whole immune system will align to fight the "common enemy."

Or you have come to realize that we are a part of nature; that we have more bacteria and fungi in our bodies than human cells. You have taken responsibility for the ecological health of your own body and you respect the delicate balance of life. You work on what you put into your body, how you treat your body, and how you manage stress because you want a resilient body, primed for what it does best: protect you from injury and acute diseases, and send you symptoms when it needs your attention. Most illness' or chronic disease has its starting point with stress. A stress that we have not been able to cope with. Since we live in a "health" culture where the majority of us are disassociated from health awareness, we are often disconnected from our bodies.

1

There are three elements needed to change our relationship with stress:

1. Truly understand stress, and its many faces
2. Understand how the body works
3. Work with your body

Let's face it, we will always have stressors; living in a glass bubble is not an option. So, it is crucial to learn how we can minimize the impact of stress. Remember, you are the one most equipped with understanding your stressors, able to decide to act and ultimately responsible for the choices you make. As physicians, we ask ourselves continually how is it we can better serve? I think, at this point, it is by encouraging prevention and turning the disease management system into a health promoting one. This changes everything.

My goal with *A Healer in Every Household: Simple Solution for Stress* is to equip the conscious consumer with a deep understanding of the basis and philosophy of medicine so that you have the framework to contextualize all approaches to health and healing. My invitation to you is to join me on this paradigm shifting journey, and invite your health care team, your doctors, your fitness trainers, your dentist, and your loved ones.

Most doctors and health care practitioners enter the field with a strong desire to help people. Many have a personal story, often of a family member or relative who suffered. Whether or not they died or were "saved," a light was turned on because of their experience. The practitioner enters the field of medicine driven by a desire to help others or find a solution to unresolved health issues.

Once this path of service is ignited, the desire to serve keeps the focus on the doctor's healing mission, despite the constant evolution and refinement of the various disciplines, specialties and solutions.

We go from avid students to established prac-titioners, becoming experts in what we hold dear — at least the lucky ones amongst us do. But many never quite reach their goal, although they fill a need (however lofty) that feels inhumane to abandon.

Despite our best intentions, at some point many of us get caught up in a system that ends up defining our practice. Right before our very eyes, patients come and go, only some of whom we have helped.

We become aware that "Dr. Google" has been diagnosing and coming up with solutions - some interesting, some frightening inspiring a new breed of patient. They nonetheless look to us for solutions, but they often leave with more questions than, answers.

Our hands are tied, our tongues silent, and our eyes,once glowing with compassion, go blank.

A New Paradigm for Health

The truth is that there is a new paradigm, which we can choose to ignore or embrace. An emerging movement of consciousness about the health of the planet, and our individual health, is empowering people to take a more active role in their health, rather than just "blindly" following the advice of their doctor or health practitioner.

As in parenting, the phrase "because I said so" is falling on deaf ears. For the "old" approach to work, a whole infrastructure is required. There must be dire consequences and disciplinary action for anyone who fails to heed the pronouncements of the authorities. Our world is changing fast.

New research in quantum physics, the development of the field of psychoneuroimmunology, and the Baby Boomers' grasp on anti-aging are just some of the forces driving the human potential for change to a whole new level.

I invite all of you to embrace, rather than resist, this change and to play your role within this evolution, rather than apart from it.

Evidence of this expanding awareness and interest in the importance of taking a proactive approach to individual health is found in the many integrative medical centers which are becoming the norm in Europe, in pharmaceutical companies' new emphasis on "natural" products, and in the myriad complementary and alternative treatments that are emerging daily.

From where has all this new awareness emerged? Is it in the broadening of our definition of what it means to be healthy?

We are no longer comfortable accepting the conventional, limited definition of health, which is defined simply as being symptom-free. Masking our symptoms no longer serves us.

Medicine is not the only field experiencing major

shifts. In fact, not one field or profession is exempt from its skeptics, philosophers, or innovators. Take the field of law, for example. As a young student, bright-eyed and bushy-tailed, I pursued a law degree because I wanted a fair world and believed that practicing law would bring about justice. I quickly became disillusioned, "politicized" by the existence of vested interests, politics, and doctrines reflecting contemporary paradigms of thought. Once determined to help "liberate" people, I became a little more humble when I realized the practice of law does not necessarily lead to justice. It often comes down to procedural loopholes or technicalities far removed from the original intention to see justice done.

A New Path

There is nothing like a disruption in your health, to spur a search for "solutions."

My personal experience, academic training, pre-med training, and a four-year, full time study in naturopathic medicine, as well as seven years of post-graduate training in homeopathic medicine and Bowen therapy, took me on a life-changing journey of discovery.

There was no clear-cut path in allopathy, naturo-pathy, homeopathy, or physical therapies, nor were any of the psychological approaches a clear solution for me. There was not one stand-alone therapy that was complete without my full presence and engagement with it. I had to overcome all my objections and look at my belief system, investigate the operating presumptions before I could "surrender" into any approach at all.

I was born an open skeptic, which really means I require proof of *everything*, in some form or another, while at the same time holding all options as equal possibilities. My driving force has always been a search for the "truth." I'd never be satisfied with treatments limited by statistical probability or research with operating models that are too limited to allow one to make an intelligent or informed decision. It had to apply to me *personally*. And thus it became evident that I found myself to be the "variable factor," the "player" that would make all the difference on how the statistic about "me" would fall.

It is with that realization that I understood that how you live is how you heal. This necessarily led to making an inventory of what I called "living" and what I wanted in my life. The more I discovered about myself, the more I appreciated my values and the pillars that they are supported on. They were fundamental to my choices and were the backbone for my commitment to the directions I took. Why this is a personal journey is because it mattered to me; there is nothing inherently right or better in those values and so my path is my own, as our patients have their own.

Not only did I overcome some serious "diseases," I became particularly attuned to both the process of disease and the process that led to health. This has become my expertise and why I'm absolutely convinced that the connection between the patient and the doctor is fundamental to this journey. We may realize, as I did, that all the healing comes from within, but as doctors we have a very important role to play in creating the best and most conducive environment for the patient to excel on their own journey.

Today, I *am* at peace with my health. I have "found myself" on this journey. I am free of scoliosis, tuberculosis, multiple sclerosis, and cancer, and I am living a life full of happiness and gratitude. I have realized that healing is really about living life with consciousness and being present. Since 1992 I've helped thousands of patients and trained hundreds of students to achieve optimum health and to engage fully in their lives.

This book is offered as a roadmap to help doctors and health care practitioners get focused and reconnect to their purpose so they can truly and fully serve their patients.

It is as well intended for you, the patient so that you can learn to be confident in trusting your own intuition and healing journey.

Subjective, Objective, Assessment, Plan

I have chosen to explore the fundamental assumptions behind the "SOAP" (Subjective, Objective, Assessment, Plan) notes traditionally used by doctors during their initial interviews with patients. The reason I felt this was important is because it is the standard structure of the interview that is held whenever a patient sees a doctor. This standard protocol is fraught with assumptions that I feel get in the way of the doctor-patient relationship if these assumptions are not examined.

First, I discuss the subjective presentation of a symptom, from its concept to its framework. We will explore what

I call the patient's "subjective" suppositions and stories.

"Subjective" is based on suppositions because what we perceive is woven out of the fabric of our reference points that determine how we interpret our experiences.

The degree of consciousness we have towards the "stories" we tell about our lives and our health ultimately determines our degree of agency in the process of healing. The account of "reality" is the result of our personal experiences, which we make sense of by reference to the conceptual framework from which we operate.

In health, the framework is the point of reference, based on conscious and unconscious extrapolations of possible etiologies and presumed outcomes.

The point is that it is in the *subjective* experience of disease and the underlying assumptions, and not in the objective findings, in which the true assessment and prescription are found. Until a time that those presumptions are clearly reflected and acknowledged by both patient and doctor and brought to consciousness, there is little support for healing. Both need to see eye to eye.

It is my experience that the subjective account of the "illness" informs the objectives of the patient and should influence the assessment choices for the prescription.

Most of our learning in the subtleties of the application of medicine will come from really listening to the patient's subjective experiences of their symptoms, and through dialogue make a subtle shift that allows for greater consciousness.

In the final analysis, our subjective worlds contain the

only "truth" we will ever know. Ultimately, all healing is self-healing.

Next, I offer an examination of the "objective" presentation, calling into question the term "objective" itself. Traditionally, it has always been regarded as scientific, showing "what is really going on." Rather than "objective," I prefer to call it "observation," for it summarizes how patients deal with their symptomatology, principally their objectives and objections.

Solutions, or "prescriptions," don't mean anything without a context; thus it is essential to get to the fundamental objectives a patient has, and the general objections and misconceptions they may feel with regard to their health.

It is evident that patients who have a broader definition of health will be looking for treatments and health care that is broader in scope and reflective of their personal attitude towards health.

This objective is framed by the patient's own definition of health. The patient's relationship to their symptoms is the biggest factor in determining their informed objectives. The spectrum ranges from perceiving symptoms as the body's enemy, to seeing them as signs that can help to refocus their lives and that are imbued with meaning and wisdom.

A more philosophical and spiritual perspective informs the relationship patients have to their symptoms. It's a perspective that's hard to capture in pill form. Even coronary heart disease can be either a prescription for heart and cholesterol medications, or a plan for exercise, healthy eating habits, lifestyle modifications and emotional insights.

For the patient, their objections to certain approaches define the way they are framing their experience and distinguishing from the elements that don't belong to their subjective assessment of that experience. For the doctor, it really comes down to being open, listening, observing, and refusing to believe one can be "objective."

Despite all "objective" findings that may be found amongst patients, including the "objective" names of the condition and their gravity, these findings have little bearing on the therapeutic outcomes. So what is "objective" about this part of the interview? "Disease calling" does not predict the outcome and may in fact reinforce the nocebo effect. Since the ultimate outcome is more closely linked to the subjective experience of the patient, why not spend more time to get to know that patient?

Taking another example, such as pain following an injury, our perception of the role and function of pain will determine how we experience the pain and what we want to do about it. The "objective" of the patient is informed by their ability to place their symptoms into a framework and context determined by their knowledge, philosophical view, spiritual understanding and critical-thinking abilities.

I believe the onus is on the doctor to inform or facilitate their patients' process. It is absurd to practice as though medicine exists in a vacuum, that it is not culturally, politically and philosophically-based.

This leads to a more fundamental question with regard to our role as doctors. Do we have a role in expanding the expectations of what it means to be healthy? Can we broaden patients' views on health, or do we succumb to being technicians in the system, merely filling prescriptions, passive enablers of the desires of our patients, the "consumer's"? Do commercial interests inform these desires? Is it our role to be educators in health care?

The next section puts "assessment" into context. It is necessarily reflective of the role we see symptoms playing in health and disease. This section explores current research in psychoneuroimmunology and pain in order to illustrate that the categories used for "diagnosis" do not reflect the whole picture, and as such cannot inform a "plan" which takes advantage of the insights of the most current research.

Assessment is crucial, as it determines the Plan. This is the place and time in which we evaluate and make sense of the entire symptomatology.

My practice has uniquely positioned me to study and extend our understanding of the various aspects that come into play in assessing the patient's symptoms.

The system of classifying and matching diseases with their "appropriate" drug-based solutions is very limited, because the patient's symptomatology may not always fit neatly within existing categories, causing real conditions to either not be treated at all, or be managed by drugs that are indicated to diminish or inhibit the symptoms.

More often that not, we witness the rough compartmentalization of the patient's body into medical subcategories.

Every body part that produces a symptom gets its own prescription, but the overall state of the patient is barely improved. Nothing reaches the underlying why behind all the accumulation of symptoms, and nothing speaks to the patient as a whole.

When we look at symptoms for example, how we assess what they mean decides in part our action plan. If symptoms are seen as an expression of the body, then we can make choices that either support the body by strengthening it, or that protect it by "attacking" the invader.

However, this goes even deeper because we may find that the disease is actually manifested by a dysfunctional internal state. And if this were true, we'd be faced with explaining how any "attack" therapy could possibly ever reinforce or strengthen the underlining terrain. Our assessment is based on what we perceive is happening, which is informed by our theoretical framework of reference based on evolving theories in science. It is the same for pain, in that we can choose either to mask it, or to look for the source (which then raises the whole psychoneuro-immunological dimension).

The Mind Body Connection

The two sections on pain and psychoneuro-immunology (PNI), the study of the mind-body connection, will highlight the limitations of the traditional Cartesian approach, which views disease as separate from the patient and calls for the arbitrary and unfounded separation of body and mind. As Plato said, "The part can never be well unless the whole is well." We will explore different scientific findings that will help you answer those questions for yourself.

Understanding the factors which may have contributed to a patient's illness can help us address and eliminate the cause, rather than merely alleviate the symptoms of a condition. The fact that the mind and body work as one, with our physical and emotional reactions intricately intertwined and affecting our neuro-immune pathways, makes it imperative for us to expand our approach to both assessment and prescription.

This necessarily includes our assessment of emotional symptoms. Do we recommend treating uncomfortable emotional states with drugs so that patients are less aware of them, or do we dig deeper and discover their real role for that person?

If we are looking at the person as a whole, then terminology is important. Emotions deemed "suppressed" are in fact just expressed in another way. The body will find a way to manifest them. So if we don't separate mind and body, not even emotional states of illness will be suppressed, just expressed in one way or another.

To reiterate, when assessing a patient's presenting symptomatology, it becomes of fundamental importance to establish what your framework or approach will be. Do we at the very least recommend our patients to explore this adventure for themselves?

Do you see the expression of their symptoms as a DSM "disease category," or as the body's cry for help? Will you categorize their symptomatology into "disease entities" which will point to prescriptions
either on the biological level (such as antibiotics and
anti-inflammatories) or emotional level (such as anti-psychotics)?

Do you fundamentally believe that the body is at war

with the environment and is being invaded, or that it's in a self-destroying war with itself? Do you believe that you are witnessing a body in need of nutritional support, emotional support, or environmental support, or maybe just a treatment that calls on the body's self-healing capacity?

And very fundamentally, behind that is the question whom are we treating ? a patient with a disease, or a disease which happens to be "attacking" that patient?

Lastly, the "plan", often reduced to the term "prescription", involves exploring the patient-doctor relationship and reaffirms the doctor's purpose by opening up the healing dialogue.

I believe that when the body produces symptoms, we need to LISTEN because it is trying to say something.

This is true of pain, inflammation, disease and even symptoms with no established category.

Cut or Burn, Bandage and Forget

If we take a more integrative approach and look at the appearance of these symptoms outside our contemporary paradigm, we would question the conventional "pragmatic" approach to cut or burn, bandage and forget, which basically decontextualizes the body from nature and meaning. Just because we don't understand the meaning these symptoms may have is no reason to create a smaller framework in diagnosis and decide on a prescription that suits only the "understood" part of the story.

It became clear to me that the "solution" for the patient

has to by necessity reflect the "problem," and if the diagnosis is not seen as the problem then how on earth could a solution for the diagnosis be of any help?

Recent research on pain and the problems encountered with the definition of chronic pain, pain management issues, and the paucity of treatment options, concludes that it is crucial for the patient to be fully engaged in their healing journey.

With regard to the experience of pain, researchers cannot link the lesion/trauma to the degree of perceived pain in a reliable way. Though we may be able to understand some of the neuronal modulations and pathways, we can only surmise the degree of sensitivity felt, and there is a big gap when it comes to "lesional proof."

Therapeutically, emphasis on pain-killers may actually miss the mark, as there is much more to the story. The best predictor of the downward transition from acute injury to chronic disability is not drug therapy, but rather maladaptive attitudes and beliefs, lack of social support, heightened emotional reactivity, substance abuse, and job dissatisfaction.

As psychoneuroimmunology offers a conceptual and biological understanding of the mind-body connections, pain and the concept of pain has evolved from a purely biomedical concept to a multi-dimensional understanding. Several authors have categorized research-based management and treatment approaches, which have given us a broader definition and understanding of pain.

An individual's beliefs about pain, emotional

experience, and pain behaviour are interrelated. Taking into account the four dimensions of pain experience (nociception, pain perception, suffering, and pain behaviour), the biopsychosocial approach to managing chronic pain is definitely an improvement over the biomedical approach.

Do Doctors Opt for the Easy "Solution"?

What role do we, as doctors, have to play in the creation of disillusioned patients suffering in pain from our failure to fully disclose the subtleties involved in dealing with it, and not just opting for the easy "solution" that is for the most part short-term and destructive?

Given the research in psychoneuroimmunology showing the importance of stress and the effects it has on the body, and the findings in pain research showing coping skills to be the most useful approach to diminishing the impact of stress, it is apparent that approaches that focus on "stress" play an important part in the health of patients.

Stress is a pervasive factor in many of our patients' lives. It has been found that individuals with high stress levels and excellent coping skills may have minimal effects from stress on the functioning of their immune systems. In contrast, low levels of stress experienced by individuals who have poor coping skills may cause significant alterations in immune functioning, increasing their susceptibility to disease. The actual amount of stress is not as important in determining its effect on the immune system as an individual's coping skills.

Thus, we must ask whether drugs can ever be subtle enough to account for such individual variations? Have we not come full circle with the understanding that the "coping" skills of the individual are paramount? If coping is the best way to alleviate the feedback loop of stress, then all our therapeutic efforts should be placed on understanding this mechanism. Have we ever looked at what increases people's coping skills? Have we ever considered how proper diet, nutrition and exercise increase people's ability to cope with stress? "Coping" is not just a mental activity. It is a biological one.

And the biology does not exist in a vacuum — our biology exists in a psycho-social, emotional and spiritual context.

We need to look at all presenting symptoms, including the story behind the parable as well as the chameleon-like nature of pain and stressors. We must be guided toward the Plan by a deep understanding and reflection with the patient on the meaning of the symptoms experienced by them.

Treating a Disease and Not the Person

A growing need for an integrative approach to health, encompassing the full understanding and commitment of the patient in their course of therapy is evident. Treating a "disease" without treating the person who developed it is pointless. The advantages of engaging patients as co-facilitators in achieving improved health far outweigh the biomedical "GP as Expert" approach. What's more, research shows the patient's increased control over their body and health yields beneficial results.

The "self-regulatory theory" is an approach to health management that strongly engages the patients' will to implement the advice given. The belief is founded on the understanding that for medical treatments to be effective, the patient needs to be interested in improving their own health.

So as a doctor, what extent of responsibility do you have in assessing the situation and exploring the possible "prescriptions"? How much of the patient's story will you relate to and what are the filters through which you will assess the choices they are making and the possible impact those choices have on their lives?

Stepping away from the simple drug prescription associated with the said diagnosis, the role the doctor plays must necessarily change. When one delves into the root causes of diseases, etiology, circumstances, aggravating factors, stressors, coping skills, psychological outlook, support systems available etc., the prescription becomes much more elaborate and individualized. What is true for one patient suffering from the same disease or ailment is not necessarily true for the other.

The Meaning of Symptoms

One of the most effective ways of helping the patient to take the steps that will help him or her gain their health back is to have them share the "meaning" of their symptoms. Implicit in the self-diagnosis is the solution. It has been my experience that patients by and large know what their problem is, how they got there and when given different options, know what course of treatment will most likely help them.

When a patient is able to gather meaning and attribute an understanding to their health status, this enhanced awareness is a high motivator to participate in their health reconstruction and improvement.

Researchers concur that what is needed is methodology that allows the person to elaborate on his personal meanings of events and the possibilities of alternative constructions.

When a person starts to comprehend her/his experience in terms of a metaphor, they find the power to create a new reality.

Thus, it appears that direct patient involvement in the process of healing, established through their own interpretation of the meaning of their symptomatology, as well as a clear visual formulation of their intention to potentiate a healing action is a "prescription" that will yield the best results. The doctor's role is to help educate and support the process.

Finding ways for patients to shift their perspectives may be one of the most powerful prescriptions for health.

It is my hope that my experience and information will enhance your own knowledge and understanding on this evolving path of awareness and service to healing and health.

If you are feeling overwhelmed by our times or distraught by this rapidly changing world and are perhaps even facing your own health challenges, I hope to offer some clarity.

Ultimately, our health is in our hands — we are not even players without it. Our goals and aspirations have led us to this service. This book offers insight and experience that can make it easy and painless for you to find your voice as a 21st century doctor.

In Health,
Dr. Manon Bolliger, ND, DHANP, FCAH, CHC, RBHT

Chapter One
Subjective: The Symptom Story

"One valuable aspect of the subjective symptom to preventive medicine lies in the ability of the patient to feel ill long before overt pathology develops. On the subjective level the patient's vital force may be less disturbed, and thus more easily cured. The homoeopath is equally at home with both sets of symptoms, and indeed usually puts greater emphasis on the subjective symptoms because many of these represent the mind of the patient, which is the most evolved and individual part. These symptoms are not unscientific to the homoeopath, because they are present in the proving of the remedies, so it is a simple matter to include them in the symptom picture without worrying about their lack of objectivity."

Principles of Homeopathic Philosophy

When interviewing a patient using the traditional SOAP format, we start with the patient's subjective presentation of symptoms.

"Subjective," as opposed to "objective," refers to the findings presented by the patient that are formed by their interpretation. Subjective implies a personal rendition, void of an "objective" or "scientific" basis. It is the account from the perspective of the patient.

The "objective" part of the SOAP format is where the doctor states the "real" findings, which most commonly represent what meets the eye, and occasionally includes a description of the presenting nature of the patient. "A mild-mannered 64-year-old widowed man is limping and favoring his right leg," would be an example. The perspective is from the doctor's point of view.

Without spending time deliberating the basis of these loosely defined and arbitrary conceptual separations, let's explore the basis of the subjective presentation of symptoms.

The subjective presentation of symptoms does not exist in a vacuum. Patients often describe what they "have" based on what they "feel" is happening, or with fear of what they "think" is happening. What they "think" is happening is based on extrapolated knowledge, partial information, or familial genetic "expectations" - basically, interpretations of what might be going on.

"I feel that there is a mass in the lower part of my abdomen. It is as if there is an obstruction." Or "I feel like there is a gaping hole in my stomach and as if my stomach is being eaten away." "My hips feel like they are being twisted and pulling my shoulders out of place." Each of these patient accounts has a sensation and gives the impression of a process.

Accompanying this process is a framework of reference, based on conscious and unconscious extrapolations of possible etiologies and outcomes. The account of "reality" is the result of our personal experiences, which we make sense of by putting into a conceptual framework. Further experiences continue to reinforce and confirm this framework, until, maybe one day something unexplained forces us out of this loop and causes us to question our assumptions.

Basically, our perceptions of what is happening are colored by our assumptions. What we believe we see and feel is reality according to us.

"Subjective" is based on suppositions because what we perceive is woven out of the fabric of our reference points that determine how we interpret our experiences.

The Doctor Knows "Best"

When some patients go to a doctor, they relinquish their own experiences to the belief that the doctor knows "best" and while seeking a diagnosis they do not feel as if they have any responsibility or input that could make a difference. On the other hand, there are those patients that want to be heard from the standpoint of their experience and/or their assumptions. So the solution they are seeking must be a solution that addresses the problem they believe needs solving.

The diagnosis, from the patient's point of view, as well as the "cure," will rest on their understanding of what "treatment" can do to help them. Before even getting to that point, it is important to realize that there is a huge range of operating assumptions on the part of the patients' participation in their health which determines the degree of importance of discovering both their "story" and the relative importance of the doctor's operating presumptions, and whether they need to be on the same page. The degree to which the patient feels they participate in this process reflects complex philosophical perspectives on life, responsibility, deference, trust in authority, understanding of healing and the desire to achieve outcomes, both consciously and unconsciously.

The degree of consciousness we have towards the "stories" we hold about our lives and our health ultimately determines our degree of agency in the process of healing.

Several patient stories illustrate my point:

The first is that of a 67-year-old female who fractured her patella bracing herself from a fall. When first interviewed, the patient had no recollection of the fall, which fractured her kneecap. In fact, upon examining her body, it was evident by the ecchymosis that she had actually fallen on her hip. The fracture was a clean, single fracture mid-way horizontally across her patella, as was evident by a gaping space separating the two parts of the fractured bone.

When given an explanation of how the fracture would have occurred, the patient experienced a clear and deliberate preference to her explanation. She was told that this was a common injury, typically seen in car accidents when the passengers tighten their quadriceps in order to brace themselves from a foreseeable accident. The break of the patella actually takes place when the femur bone breaks it in half as the quadriceps retract over the bony protuberance.

The patient had two objections to the situation. The first is that because what happened had been so shocking, the idea of it being a simple or common fracture was not congruent with her experience of the situation. The shock and disbelief that the injury was "so stupid, so unnecessary, that it complicated her life so tremendously," and "made her so dependent" were all thoughts incongruent and inconsistent with statements such as: "If you were going to fracture your patella, that was the best fracture to get," and "Your body will heal this in a matter of weeks."

The second objection is that the body, in this case the musculature of the body, would not "naturally" harm itself. It was inconceivable that her body would do such a thing and as such, the "story" of the accident changed from its original amnesia of how the incident took place, to an elaborate description of falling smack right into the patella with the possibility of a compound fracture and even complications in healing due to inflammatory responses and infection.

One can wonder what the probable outcome is of the healing of this simple fracture in this patient, compared to the identical fracture in a patient who felt so blessed and grateful to have come out alive in a head-on collision and "only have a simple and clean fracture" to contend with.

The value of the subjective rendition is at least as important as the X-rays (which would represent the Objective findings in this particular case).

Looking at the hospital procedures, we find the first thing this patient was offered, according to common practice, was morphine for the "pain." When she stated that she had no actual pain, she was told to take it to avoid the pain that would ensue. As she was four days awaiting her surgery (her injury not being considered an emergency) she kept wondering when to expect the pain.

She was then offered oxycodone as a weaker pain drug. When she was informed from another source that this drug was highly addictive and coated with codeine she opted out, as she did not want to exacerbate her already existing constipation. This decision was "allowed" by the nurse and was included in the file as if she had taken all prescribed medications.

She ended up taking nothing other than two doses of extra strength Tylenol and Arnica Montana (a homeopathic remedy) prescribed for trauma following surgery. When she enquired whether it was normal to have no pain, she received varying responses, ranging from "We always give morphine," to "I don't know, it never comes up. We automatically put it into the IV drip."

The clear presumption of this standard practice is that all fractures are painful and require painkillers. So it's standard practice: the subjective experience of the patient does not alter the automatic Objective annotations, the Assessment or the Plan.

Why? Because the experience of the patient is regarded as less relevant or important than the general presumptions gathered by "objective" findings representing this type of scenario.

What is missed altogether, but which factors most strongly, is the psychological discomforts from the trauma, which were excluded from the history and yet played the most significant role in this patient's "unexpected" slow recovery. This patient was never met at the level of her experience of the subjective symptoms she presented with. In fact, the complete denial of her experience and the blind "normal procedures" hampered her recovery, as some part of her has attached meaning to the injury and has managed to create ongoing inflammation and loss of range of motion. It is clear that the subjective experience is a relevant one and plays a prime role in the outcome. A more conscious and cognizant of this phenomena approach in relationship with the nurses, doctors and hospital department may have produced a very different outcome for this "objective" fracture.

The second story is that of the different presentations of mobility issues I have seen with patients affected with the sequelae of polio. Both received the same treatment. I treated them both with a technique called BowenFirst™, a physical therapy I use extensively in my practice.

What is BowenFirst™ ?

BowenFirst™ is like a "body language translator" that allows the therapist to follow the signals the body is giving. Bowen Therapy was originally conceived of and named after the late Tom Bowen(1916-1982) of Geelong, Victoria in Australia. This myofascial manipulation technique has evolved over the years through its many proponents and varies from simplistic bodywork therapy to wholistic integrated therapy, which incorporates the advances in brain research (Such as BowenFirst™).

This therapy involves using gentle touch to allow the body to let go of its "stuck" patterns of pain and restriction. It is as though, in a self-protective effort, which at first may have been warranted, the body gets "stuck" protecting the body part with pain, calcification, inflammation or swelling—all attempts to immobilize the damaged joint. The pattern outlives the actual damage, and thus necessitating de-programming of the pain pathways and encouraging a healthy healing response.

Each treatment consists of various sets of moves on muscle, nerves and tendons, interspersed by short pauses that allow the body to integrate the effects.

BowenFirst™ is a therapeutic technique that helps the body disengage from stress and the fight or flight response and switch the patient into parasympathetic mode, allowing rest, digestion, proper respiratory patterns and healing to ensue.

By directly activating the nervous system, the body is then able to trigger changes both physically as well as emotionally.

Muscles can reflect stress by becoming shorter, tense and spasmodic, but they also hold unto chemical mediators that are responsible for our emotions. This is why, when patients feel better after treatment, the spasm releases but so do the emotions carried with them. Upledger (see note) has refereed to this process as a somatoemotional release." BowenFirst™ therapy's gentle resetting of the physical body encourages the brain and fascial network to integrate selecting a more optimal "blueprint."

In just 3 to 5 sessions, most patients experience relief. The treatment is gentle, does not require effort on the part of the patient, and yields results of 50% to 80% improvement by the third session and 100% by the fifth session in 85% of patients.

In patients who have been on strong opioids, like morphine, results are varied, possibly because they have reduced sensitivity to experience the input from the treatment. Patients taking muscle relaxants or using methods that artificially and temporarily achieve a short-term functional goal, i.e., relaxing the muscle without teaching the muscle how to relax on its own, may require additional treatments to see results, however, most patients have a very quick turn-around period.

As BowenFirst™ is a fairly new approach, the mechanisms of its actions are not all understood. Research would be very welcome as it would allow patients to understand the mechanisms involved and seek some comfort in what at this point appears to many as a "miracle." The current scientific research on pain sheds some light on the subject.

**Compare these two patients'
experience of the same "diagnosis":**

The first is a male who had been afflicted by polio as a child, and then had to nurse his wife, who was diagnosed with Alzheimer's. Objectively, his left leg had flaccid muscles and was two-thirds the size of his right leg. When he first came to me as a patient, he only had one mission. His goal was to improve his gait so that he would not suffer from back pain and be better able to help his wife.

He saw me a few times at first, and then only once every eight months or so. Not only did he not suffer from back pain, his gait corrected itself and his flaccid leg was able to act "as if" it were entirely normal.

The other patient was a female, also afflicted by polio in her early years. In her case, though, she appeared to have no flaccidity and the nerve conduction was unaffected by the polio. Her goal was to be able to walk "normally" and to finally meet a "proper" man, not one she had to endure or put up with "because of" her condition.

After her treatment, her musculature was able to perform all parts of a normal gait and her potential for permanent recovery was evident. She, however, did not recover, and her exaggerated gait reinforced her perceived misfortune in life. She would not get the man she "deserved," as she was a victim of polio. Her understanding of the incurable nature of polio and the reliance on her "story" as a "victim" may have contributed.

The point is that it is in the subjective experience of her disease and the underlying assumptions, and not in the objective findings, that the true assessment and prescription are found. Until a time that her presumptions are clearly reflected back to her and brought to consciousness, there is no room for recovery.

Now, I am in no position to comment on these so-called "improper men" as I have not met them, but the underlying presumption she has about her condition and the kind of men it attracts is not factual at all. The only pattern she sees are the ones in her own mind, likely based on her lack of self-worth triggered by her interpretation of her encounter with this disease.

My point in comparing these two scenarios is that the objective label of the condition and its gravity have little bearing on the outcome. Additionally, the actual treatment used had little bearing.

The third experience I want to share are the results of my treating patients who have been diagnosed with Multiple Sclerosis (MS). I have been very favorably influenced by the work of Dr. Andre Saine, ND, my mentor in homeopathic medicine. Between his personal experience of treating this disease and his research in the literature of hundreds of successful cures, I had very clear guidelines for "expected" results. The disease could be reversed in its entirety, provided the affected limbs had not experienced demyelination with observable symptomatology for at least one full year. Even years later, and past acute optic neuritis, all symptoms of the disease would appear to be either "dormant" or non-manifest when treated appropriately.

Very early on in my practice, I saw a patient who was a psychologist and had developed MS six months prior. She had heard of homeopathy and was referred to me by a friend who had been treated by Dr. Jost Kunsli, a famous medical doctor in Germany who practiced homeopathy and made significant contributions to the profession. This patient's early onset MS was aggressive in nature, but she appeared well disposed to overcome this obstacle.

She arrived in a wheelchair, guided in by her husband, who was also a patient of mine. I conducted a 2-hour interview and felt fairly certain of the remedy I had come up with. A mere six weeks after beginning the treatment, she was out of her wheelchair and dancing.

News of her improvement spread throughout the community, despite the somewhat skeptical statements by her medical doctor inferring that she had simply had a spontaneous remission.

She was clearly of another opinion. Her experience of MS had allowed her to reconnect with her husband, who confessed he had had an affair and had been taking her for granted. When she developed this disease, he blamed himself and promised that he would make it up to her. He ran all the errands, told her she no longer needed to work, and that he would take care of her. As she had been the main caregiver throughout her life, these changes were most welcome.

Yet when I saw her at her two-month follow-up appointment, she walked in with a cane. I asked her whether she had repeated her remedy, as it looked to me that she was in a state of relapse. She cried, "If that's what it takes to have my husband look after me, then it is worth keeping the disease!"

She had noticed that as she recovered her husband had started to detach from her again as he liberated himself from the guilt he was experiencing. She felt that the only way to maintain their connection was to maintain her disease. Despite my counseling her differently, and despite her own training, this disease was going to serve her purposes, and so she refused to take any more remedy.

Not all patients will be so clear about their unconscious driving forces. Many will be driven by unquestioned or unconscious motives. And yet, when they seek your help, what is the most beneficial approach? It became clear to me that the "solution" had to reflect the "problem," and if the diagnosis was not seen as the problem then how on earth could a solution for the diagnosis be of any help?

This patient's problem was her attachment to the positive effects of her inability to look after others due to her new restrictions. She was using the consequences of the disease to achieve her stated goal. It seems clear that if she had been offered one of the many experimental drugs for MS, her situation would still be the same – she would never comply, and so the specificity of the treatment would miss the mark.

Another patient diagnosed with MS came to see me when she heard of the results her friend with Fibromyalgia had received with BowenFirst™. She had developed MS, which affected the left side of her body as well as her face, which had partial paralysis. She came in with a limp and dragged the left side of her body like a heavy, limp rag.

Having researched some of the available treatments for MS, she was reticent to use any of the experimental drugs due to their side effects. I advised her to try homeopathic medicine, based on my clinical experience at the time and my personal results, but she wanted BowenFirst™. I had not as yet treated MS using this method, but nonetheless, for my own peace of mind, I conducted my usual 2-hour homeopathic interview in order to collect all the history and symptomatology necessary and then proceeded to perform my work.

It became apparent in her interview that the patient's MS started following an accident in which she fell off her horse and broke her ankle. I proceeded to treat and address the weakness in her left side, which allowed her to leave the office without using her cane. I addressed her facial paralysis, and in four sessions during one month she was free of any apparent symptoms of MS.

She returned one month later, still greatly improved, but now with her ankle acting up for the first time since her surgery. I proceeded to treat her again and addressed this old injury. What she shared with me at that moment had a huge impact on my practice and my way of looking at healing. She told me that her ankle "needed to be heard," and that is why it acted up. Her cure would not be complete until the original step of the spiral had been addressed.

Her perception of MS as a disease originating from a fall led to her insight about how to treat it. She was not interested in "internal medicine," whether it is homeopathy or experimental drugs. A sugar pill of any sort could not answer what felt to her the need for a hands-on approach.

She wanted a physical-based treatment that had the capacity to address both the shock and trauma element she had experienced, as well as the physical ramifications of the original "causative" injury. Her subjective account informed her objectives, ie. her treatment goals and assessment choices for the prescription of her choice. I delivered the goods—she mastered her body's ability to heal.

The statement, "my ankle needed to be heard" confirmed once and for all that your patients are really your best teachers and that most of the learning in the subtleties of the application of medicine comes from really listening to the patient's experiences of their symptoms.

Reboot Your Body

In this chapter, I will give you a practical overview of stress and its impact on you and your family, ensuring that you understand how powerful the body is. My goal is to have you seriously empowered to consider yourself to be the Healer in Your Household. Read through this chapter and join me to gain further clarity on how you can start implementing an "at home version" of BowenFirst™ therapy: what I call Reboot Your Body. Meanwhile, allow me to share with you why working through the body to calm the mind is not only essential but so extraordinarily effective.

What is stress for you?

For most people, stress is a state of mental or emotional strain or tension resulting from adverse or demanding circumstances. Identifiable signs of stress include indigestion, bloating, constipation, nervousness, anxiety, sleeplessness, irritability, and impatience. Let's look at factors that might be the root cause of stress.

There are 4 categories of stress:

1. Mental stress. This stress frequently results from pressures to meet deadlines. It's useful to distinguish between positive and negative stress. The former can be productive, allowing us to focus on problems at hand and to motivate us to meet deadlines. Negative mental stress is not productive and when it becomes chronic it

contributes to reduced health. Negative stress can also give rise to poor, insufficiently considered, decision making.

2. Physical stress. It is valuable to distinguish between acute and chronic physical stress. Acute physical stress is caused by exercise. The long-term benefits are valuable, but muscles need to be gradually built up to avoid injury. Chronic physical pain is a sign of distress in the body. While there may be some temporary pain from acute stress, under chronic stress the pain does not abate. When people experience poor health outcomes, such as pain, it is often assumed that the root cause of the distress is the pain. That pain could be though just the symptom of a stressful situation which needs to be addressed. Trying to resolve the problem with pain killers only camouflages the symptoms.

3. Physiological stress. Acute physiological stress can create happy hormones. These are the kind of hormones a woman's system would be flooded with the type of stress that results from giving birth to a baby. Again, there are acute and chronic versions of this kind of stress. Chronic physiological stress is created when strain is put on the body, such as through inadequate sleep. Physiological stress can take a toll on your body over the long term. Chronic physiological stress leads to many common health problems, including in areas of mental, cardiovascular, and immune health. It can inhibit our ability to heal and sleep. It can impact our fascia and make us more prone to disease.

4. Emotional stress. This stress can be separated into the categories of worry and grief. Worry is the stress we feel when concerned about our ability to pay our bills during a crisis or how contagious are those around us when we're out in public. Grief is the kind of stress experienced at a time of tragedy, such as with the death of a loved one. Regret or helplessness are examples of grief stress, wondering if other choices by us could have avoided the tragic outcome.

Among people with poor coping skills, ongoing emotional stressors take a toll on the body. Even low levels of stress can compromise immune function, increasing disease susceptibility. Anxiety, insomnia, indigestion all can be aggravated by stress. Hormone levels can be disrupted by stress, as well. The likelihood of experiencing chronic disease can be increased by persistent stress.

Stress, for instance, damages the gut, leading to increased toxins and inflammation. This can decrease liver function, leading to systemic inflammation and adrenal burn-out. Additionally, gut damage causes toxicity to the vagus nerve, which also affects the liver. The resulting decrease in liver function results in increased gas, bloating, and constipation, as well as decreased bile and digestion, all leading to chronic inflammation. This effect, known as the gut-liver adrenal connection, stresses the adrenal glands, leading down a path to burn out.

Of central important to avoid these types of outcomes is the ability to cope with stress. A positive feedback loop is involved. Coping with emotional stress reduces the stress on your body. This allows you maintain a healthier body, which in turn helps you deal better with your emotional stress. It is important to appreciate that coping is not merely a mental activity; it has important physiological implications. Your thoughts, including your capacity to cope, directly affects your body.

Survival mode is not a healing mode

Living in a constant state of fear can cause havoc. This is a situation seen regularly, as when patients wait for test results, which often present false positives. Healing itself is not a fear-based activity. We are wired to protect ourselves for survival, which is all part of the fight-or-flight mechanism. That is our sympathetic nervous system going into overdrive.

The truth is that it is possible that you believe you are "coping," and yet your body is not. Your body may well have another rendition of reality. We have the uncanny ability to delude ourselves consciously. When we include the programs that run in the background, in our subconscious, they may be causing us stress only our body has tapped into. I had the belief that I was strong enough to withstand a very difficult relationship. My compassion and strength and optimistic view of the world did not prevent my body succumbing to the impact of the stress. I will share later what my path to recovery was and how I got my health back because, in fact the entire process is a whole other book. Suffice it to say that we need to ensure that "coping" is not just a mental construct, but that it is felt in every cell of our body. Until you have done the work of considering the impact of your thoughts and beliefs, the most effective way to de-stress your body is to deeply connect with it. That is why practices like meditation and yoga are crucial, and so is Reboot Your Body.

I ask you to keep an open learner's mind; be inquisitive and become aware of what you are thinking. And, when you start to experience this work, reflect upon what you are feeling. What I am asking of you is a paradigm shift. Like Albert Einstein said: "Problems cannot be solved with the same mindset that created them."

When addressing chronic or autoimmune disease, pain, injury, or trauma, it is essential to look at the key operational systems in our body. In later chapters we'll go into more depth on the parasympathetic system, vagus nerve, the gut-liver-adrenal connection as well as the ventral and dorsal aspects of the vagus nerve. It is important that you are thoroughly informed about your physiology, by understanding the hypothalamic-pituitary-adrenal axis. This helps us better understand how our body functions and our immune system operates. But let's start with the basics.

Stress response, colloquially known as the "fight-or-flight" response, is our body's emergency reaction system. This system generates hormones that give us extra speed if we have to run away from a bear. It is designed to keep us safe in emergency situations.

However, the stress response can work against you. You can turn it on when you don't really need it. As a result, your body can perceive an emergency where there's none. This misfiring can release unnecessarily high levels of cortisol and adrenaline, causing symptoms such as:

1. Weight gain, mainly fat on your belly and upper back
2. High blood pressure
3. Severe fatigue
4. Insomnia
5. Irritability
6. Difficulty concentrating
7. Muscle weakness
8. and more....

Stress has different sources. As mentioned above, thinking affects your stress. There are objective facts we need to accept, but our interpretation of those facts makes all the difference to our stress levels. When you believe that challenges can be overcome, your behavior matters, and change is possible, you thrive. This approach manages the automatic stress response that could otherwise damage your health. This again is the positive feedback loop between mental and physical stress. This is the reason that there is a limit to the impact that cognitive therapy can have on stress. It's also why high blood pressure cannot be easily managed with behavioural therapies.

Stress is perceived by the body in direct proportion to the balance of our stress hormones. When your body's stress hormones are elevated – e.g., by an increase in cortisol, adrenaline, or norepinephrine levels – you experience negative emotions. On the other hand, when you serotonin or dopamine levels increase, you experience positive emotions. Balancing the autonomic nervous system allows the body to recalibrate, blood pressure to normalize, and infuses a healthy injection into that positive feedback loop.

Sometimes stress triggers PTSD. At those times knowing how to use body-based, somatic responses is essential for modulating the "activation stress" and preventing it pushing past the tipping point. It has also been well documented that physical exercise decreases stress, as well as yoga and meditation. In short, it is through the "felt body experience" that we can best reduce physiological stress. This is related to stress regulation through proper oxygenation. Hence, breathing exercises are suggested for stress and anxiety.

Let's review the autonomic nervous system: sympathetic and parasympathetic

The autonomic nervous system is responsible for all the involuntary processes in the body: e.g., your heartbeat, breathe, and digestion. You don't need to attend those bodily functions; they respond automatically. In fact, your body responds to chemical signals that it produces. You don't need to tell your gall bladder to emulsify the chunk of food you just ate or your stomach to release gastric acids. It just works in the background. The autonomic nervous system has two branches.

The sympathetic system is our fight-or-flight system: our survival mechanism. The parasympathetic is our rest and digest system, mediated through the vagus nerve. It helps decrease heart and breathe rate, increase blood flow and digestion in our stomach, our small intestine, large intestine, pancreas, liver, and gallbladder.

It helps the spleen filter the blood, and our kidney filter out the blood and the water.

All this helps us recover and restore our health. That is the parasympathetic component represented by the ventral branch of the vagus nerve. The vagus nerve has two branches and is found on both sides of the body going through the carotid sheath, sending information to and from the heart, lying beside the carotid artery and jugular vein. It then has branches going to every internal organ: the lungs, heart, pancreas, liver, kidney, stomach, and gut.

The vagus nerve tells the brains what is happening in the organs. This is known as the gut-brain connection. The vagus nerve originates at the 10th cranial nerve and is the only nerve that leaves the cranium to connect to every organ in the chest and abdomen. Eighty percent of all information reaching the brain is afferent, meaning it comes from the organs to the brain, and 20 percent is efferent, coming from the brain to the organs (with 5 percent going to the back of the throat and the inner ear). When the brain is determining what efferent signals it needs to emit, it takes the pulse of the information provided by the organs. So, what is happening to our organs?

Dr. Stephen Porges, a developer of Polyvagal Theory, explains our nervous system's response to stress or danger. It is a three-part, hierarchical system: 1) ventral vagus activation (relaxation and social engagement); 2) sympathetic activation (fight-or-flight); and 3) dorsal vagus activation (immobilization or freeze). It is the Dorsal Vagus Complex (DVC), the more primitive unmyelinated branch of the vagus nerve and its activation, that is known as the "freeze" response. The Ventral Vagus Complex (VVC) is the newer, myelinated branch of the vagus nerve, developed in mammals, known as the social engagement system. It is our "check in" system: a social monitoring system which is currently being highly activated by the media coverage and political lobbyist handling the pandemic of 2020.

Let's look at how we operate in non-stressful situations

During non-stressful situations, if we are emotionally healthy, our bodies stay in a social engagement state: i.e., a happy, normal, relaxed state. In this state, we can connect with another human being. The parasympathetic is the rest, digest, detoxify and heal system, on one hand, and also the freeze response, on the other hand. So, we've got this ventral Vegas complex, which is also known as a social nervous system, that when engaged allows us better self-regulation. We make better decisions. We can read other people's facial expressions and better connect with them. We can accurately assess whether somebody may be afraid.

The sympathetic nervous system is our immediate reaction to stress. It affects nearly every organ in the body. The resulting fight-or-flight state is designed to keep us alive. In fight-or-flight, at some level, we believe we can still survive the threat we are facing in that moment. When our sympathetic nervous system kicks into overdrive, and we still can't escape, the dorsal vagal parasympathetic nervous system, referred to as the dorsal vagal response, takes control. As a form of self-preservation, it causes freezing or shutdown: e.g. someone might pass out under extreme stress or freeze on stage, unable to get out their words.

The challenge is that our nervous system can perceive danger where none exists. This reaction can be the result of early life exposure to stress and conditioning. When we have experienced early childhood trauma, we are sensitized to increased activation of the ventral branch of the vagus system. This response puts us on higher alert, impacting our response to social engagement cues. This sensitized state often signals externally that we are stressed and can't relax. It is a vicious circle of discordance. To demonstrate this point, say your child is afraid of dogs, and then approaches the dog with fear, the dog will pick this up and sensing your fear will engage its own survival instinct and become more alert and more likely to attack.

When we are healthy and our vagus nerve is intact and we're socially engaged. Say you are walking down the street. You smile at someone; they reciprocate, and you can walk past, thinking nothing of it. If though your body detects that things are not fine, say your nervous system gives you a cue that something is not quite right about this individual, if the nervous system is switched on, using various indices or sensory stimuli you feel a sense of warning. Bits of information are being unconsciously processed to generate that warning. When you detect this person as a threat, the fight or flight response engages. You quickly then decide. Are you going to run away, to save your skin? Or are you going to fight this person? If this cognitive process concludes, though, that you cannot fight or flee, then your dorsal vagus system kicks in and you freeze. It's called a hypo metabolic state or hibernation. Animals are wired to "play dead" and so are we.

If, however, we have experienced trauma in our past, the dorsal vagal response is more apt to fire and is often provoked by situations that do not warrant it. A general definition of trauma is: something that triggers an overwhelming mechanism in you. It is often something that feels like it is too much, too fast, too soon. First the body responds by hyper-arousal. This is sympathetic overdrive, fight-or-flight, and then goes into hypo-arousal: the freeze and faint reaction. To put an end to this response, we need to put on the dorsal vagal break. This can be achieved by reminding the body that the emergency is over.

Certain people with chronic diseases such as fibromyalgia or chronic fatigue tend to experience more this complete shutdown response. They're overstimulated, pushing them into this shutdown state.

So, you can see the importance of the vagus nerve and its many different bodily functions.

How does the Vagus nerve affect inflammation?

Chronic inflammation is associated with pretty much every chronic illness. Research shows that those with inflammatory conditions, such as rheumatoid arthritis, fibromyalgia, etc. often have decreased heart rate variability, which is a marker of reduced vagal tone. This is associated with high levels of pro-inflammatory cytokines and an increase in sympathetic nervous system activity and stress hormones, which contributes to systemic inflammation.

It is the Vagus nerve that controls inflammation through the cholinergic anti-inflammatory system. The cholinergic anti-inflammatory efferent portion of the vagus nerve comprises 15% of the efferent nerve signals which put a brake on inflammation. The brain sends messages to the gut to reduce inflammation through acetylcholine to the spleen, decreasing macrophage activity, etc. The problem is that, if there is chronic inflammation, because of bacteria or yeast that should not be there, the vagus nerve overreacts, overwhelming the slow-down mechanism of the efferent vagus nerve pathways.

The spiraling of unresolved stress to chronic disease

Every organ is affected over time. If toxins build up, they cause decrease of liver function and glutathione levels. The liver has 500 different functions. It is a master organ: our filter and detox pathway. It is our blood sugar monitor. It is of critical importance because the liver communicates with the brain. Accumulation of toxins decreases liver function. Over time, we see lowered levels of glutathione, our major antioxidant.

Blood sugar balance is monitored by the liver. If the liver can't send signals to the brain, it can't tell the brain to send information to the pancreas that releases insulin for bringing sugar into the cells. The vagus nerve ensures that the function of insulin is optimal so that when sugar is high, the liver can send signals to address it. If the liver can't do so, eventually it leads to insulin resistance.

Now, to be clear, when our bodies are under stress, we produce hormones like cortisol. Cortisol is important. It comes from the adrenal glands and its major function is to help us handle stress by increasing blood sugar levels. It signals the liver to increase glucose in the bloodstream. Cortisol helps the body manage how it uses macronutrients, protein fat and CHO. It also keeps inflammation down, regulates BP, controls sleep and wake cycles and boosts our energy.

Therefore increased stress increases cortisol and blood sugar. Add to that, if we are eating badly, our pancreas can no longer do the job of pumping enough insulin to keep the sugar levels at bay. This creates a vicious cycle: the pancreas no longer able to handle the production of insulin, the cells unable to take any more glucose, and the vagus nerve no longer able to regulate this vicious cycle. In response, the body converts glucose into fat. The result is Type 2 Diabetes, insulin resistance, metabolic disease, fatty liver, etc.

How does this impact our immune system?

For ideal stomach digestive function, we need to produce stomach acid. If stomach acid production is not functioning properly, we can't produce enough intrinsic factor, we don't have optimal peristalsis, and we lack good flora information from gut to brain. Let's not forget that 70 percent of our immune system cells are in our gut. When our body produces inflammation – in response to bacteria, fungus, yeast, toxins, etc. – it becomes overwhelmed. Chronic inflammation sets in and becomes problematic. Poor vagus nerve function causes the stress that suppresses stomach acid and digestive enzyme production, increases gut permeability (leaky gut), reduces the Migrating Motor Complex (this is the main cause of SIBO), and contributes to dysbiosis and nutrient malabsorption.

But how does the gut become so dysregulated?

Mental stress contributes to our inability to modulate physical or emotional stress. You might be getting a glimpse of what scientists meant when they coined the term: Psycho-neuro-immunology." Stress mode leads to disease: thoughts that affect the brain, hormones, the nervous system and the immune system. Thoughts have power; the answer is in the body.

Mental health diagnoses can look very similar. Maybe your condition stems from events from your past, some maybe even subconscious. Maybe you were in a bad relationship or experienced some traumatic event. Medical professionals may have told you that you can use drugs to turn down the symptoms manifesting from the accumulation of these events. The trauma is still there, though, under the surface, waiting to attach itself to new memories and experiences. You might believe your emotional or mental pain is acceptable, or somehow deserved and that it is a part of you. It may be so ingrained in your mental and physiological memory that you hardly notice the effects it has on your life, and your day-to-day well-being.

That is why, before cycling down that difficult pathway, it is important to address the body's habit of stress and how to Reboot back to peace. We know that correct breathing exercises, relaxation techniques, stress management, regular exercise and diet can help restore a person to a more peaceful state. Reboot is also a marvelous tool to help people achieve this state.

How can you measure your vagus nerve function?

Failure to self-regulate is what brings on disease as well as all the problems with the inability to modulate emotions. Ongoing stress deleteriously affects our Heart Rate Variability (HRV), leading to disease. We may have an underperforming, depleted nervous system, showing up in low HRV, or lack the capacity to self-inhibit, which has everything to do with HRV. In either case, HRV is central to the story. The HRV is affected by the health of the neuro-brain-heart axis.

Heart rhythm changes: the observed pattern can be correlated to emotional states. Distorted heart rhythm correlates with anger and emotional upsets. Whereas feelings like love and compassion correlate with a coherent pattern. Heart rate variability reflects nervous system adaptability. As PhD and author, Kelly McGonigal, writes in The Upside of Stress, compassion changes HRV because it does not activate survival and is tied into our reward system.

HRV is a major way by which we measure vagus nerve function. Higher vagal tone reflects a body that is in balance. Compassion allows you to create enhanced vagal tone. As well, vagal tone is a resource that makes it easier to tap into compassion. According to McGonigal, having low vagal tone is also a reflection of your belief about the world. If you don't believe that the world is safe, then you have a vagal tone more primed for defense.

Increased vagal tone is also associated with increased

feelings of joy and well-being, and a greater feeling of connection with others. This was the first time it's been validated that vagal tone is changed by your emotional state. So, we have an absolute correlation between heart rate variability and the emotional state. As Howard Martin, Author and Business Leader of Heart Math says: **"Much like the electricity changed the outer world, learning to harness the power and intelligence of the heart can change our inner world."** Having researched the topic for at least 30 years, have found about a 75 percent correlation between heart rate variability patterns and emotional states. I believe, a skilled practitioner could identify your emotional state through examining your heart rate variability.

Coherence reflects the neural activity synchronicity within our brain and nervous system. More information comes from the heart to the brain than the other way around. Approximately 400 studies have been published showing the impact of the lack of coordination and harmony on our health.

Why work with your body?

There is something like 600,000 signals that travel from the brain into the body every second. These signals are then routed back to the brain with information. This information is then interpreted and sent back out. Whenever we feel, hear, see, or even think: the brain uses our past experiences to process and categorize the sensation and create and delegate an appropriate response.

Cell memory structures this circuit between our brains and the soft tissues in our bodies. It provides a valuable insight into trauma. All the information of our experiences is stored in our body, in our brains certainly, but also in our cell memory. Any trauma we have experienced could still be resonating in our bodies – whether it was physical trauma, like an accident, emotional trauma, like a break-up, or mental trauma, like the psychological impact of abuse.

This cell memory forms a memory pool, filled with the details of what happened, mixed with the brain's survival mechanism and a swirl of emotions. I have found that both the body and the brain catalogue the events of physical or emotional trauma, as well as the fight-flight-or-freeze state, and the emotions that accompany them. This occurs in the neural interpretation networks of both the body and the brain.

Now for the bigger picture - the role of fascia

Touch is vital to a person's well-being, physical and emotional. Skin covers the largest surface of our body and it's the main point of contact between people. What might be less obvious is that the skin is embedded in the fascia. Some consider skin as the outermost layer of the fascia, although the fascia itself doesn't have layers because it's a matrix. Fascia is a fatty, yellow connective tissue that runs under the entire skin and covers all of the organs.

In a dead person, the fascia becomes flat and stringy — looking unimportant. It's easy to see how researchers, looking at cadavers, could dismiss it. However, the fascia has a crystalline structure, like many hexagons, stacked together. In a living person, this tissue is filled with body fluids and forms a cushion that can stretch and move almost like a soft, squishy balloon.

Anatomically, the fascia is the connective tissue below the skin, which surrounds all our organs and muscles from head to toe. Fascia has its own nervous and electrical components which create instant communication. Structurally, the fascia keeps muscles and bones in a state of buoyancy. It enables our experience of enteroception, a sense of how our body feels, and proprioception, which is our sense of positioning in space.

Our body is like an orchestra, a medical orchestra which plays a perfect symphony under the leadership of the conductor. That conductor is the fascia. It fine-tunes every instrument. It's like a biological nternet of connectivity. It circulates biological, chemical, and emotional information throughout the entire body so that our body can repair. From this perspective, you can see that your body is smarter than you think.

The fascia has largely been ignored by conventional medicine, doctors, and by us – custodians of our own bodies. This is what needs to change if we aspire to merge the mind and the body in our healing journey.

Our body is programmed to heal. We just need to reboot it.

Dr. Robert Schleip has bluntly identified the importance of the fascia: "Fascia is on the short list of the most important organs for survival." This is particularly so as it relates to matters of chronic pain. Pain is multidimensional because that's the nature of human beings. It hurts in the tissues, but the problem is in the nervous system and the fascia. Tissue may take time to get back to normal, but pain disappears when your body no longer needs to protect itself. That is the key.

Chapter Two

Objective: Observation of the Patient Objectives and Objections

"The position of an observer will influence the phenomenon being observed and affect the results of the observation."
Einstein's Theory of Relativity

In the last chapter, we looked at the Subjective portion of the SOAP formula and noted that patients always speak from the point of view of their subjective experience, which is coloured by their understanding of health and illness, their philosophy of life, and the attitudes they have toward agency.

The "O" in the standard SOAP formula stands for "Objective." The doctor needs to accurately understand the patient's subjective vision of their condition, while also recording the objective findings. The cases in the prior chapter show that this is no small task.

What are the criteria for the Objective? Except maybe for positive lab findings and physical aspects noted, any other findings would indeed be quite subjective on the part of the doctor.

First, I suggest that we demystify the term "Objective" and use "Observation," which at least implies a subjective process. Second, and I believe more usefully, would be to revise the "O" to include the Observation of the objectives of the patient and their objections.

As we saw in the last section, the objective of the first patient with MS was to keep her husband in spite of her health. She was clearly not willing to investigate the nature of their relationship and how that impacted on her health. She had the belief, that so long as she kept him in a state of guilt, she would be happy and therefor safe. She used the relationship and what he could offer her coming from a place of guilt, to "deal" with her overly accommodating and self-sacrificing self.

MS is the manifestation her healing path presented her with, and for whatever reason, she chose to look at very short term "benefits." The underlining problem is not addressed and at some point or another the chosen strategy would almost predictably fail.

In light of the objective of the patient, what is the role of the doctor? Does he/she see MS as the problem? And find a solution for the MS? To what extent do we need to take a broader perspective in our interview process and in the relationship to our patients and clarify the merits of their objectives. As you can well imagine, this two-way tango is a dance of systems of belief and consciousness. How can we address a "disease" without addressing the person who manifests this state?

When it comes to "objections," it's the same. What may seem as a long shot possibility for the patient may not be shared by the doctor. Too often though, it is the other way around. It is the doctor's lack of openness to observable phenomena around him/her because it lies outside the limited medical scope they have been accustomed to. This is probably the biggest disconnect today, in that through the internet, people share the everyday miracles they experience and it is important to work with that reality and not against it.

For the patient, their objections define the way they are framing their experience and distinguishing from the elements that don't belong there in the subjective assessment of their own experience. For the doctor, it really comes down to being open and listening-observing and not believing anyone can be "objective."

The physician and stress researcher Hans Selye wrote in *The Stress of Life*, "Most people do not fully realize to what extent the spirit of scientific research and the lessons learned from it depend upon the personal viewpoints of the discoverers. In an age so largely dependent upon science and scientists, this fundamental point deserves special attention."

There is much to be gathered in the subjective rendition of the patient's symptoms, as well as in their objectives and the objections they hold.

Finding the Objectives of the Patient

As a doctor, understanding the reason why a patient comes to you is paramount. The root of the word "doctor" means "to educate" but this part often falls short of the mandate. We must educate the patient about their symptoms, as well as the possible causes and all the options available to address them. Solutions or "prescriptions" don't mean anything without a context; thus getting to the fundamental objectives a patient has, and the general objections and misconceptions they may feel with regard to health, is essential.

A central and common "objective" a patient has when presenting with symptoms is the restoration of their health. This objective is framed by the patient's own definition of health, which we will explore.

The World Health Organization (WHO) defines health as "a state of complete physical, mental and social well-being and not merely the absence of disease or infirmity."

Interesting to note is that most of our health industry does not define health like the WHO.

The majority of financial assets in the health industry are owned by Big Pharma, which by necessity operate on the restricted "symptom-free" definition of health. A more cynical perspective would be to say that this is true outside of the sick-making industry of iatrogenic causes of illness. To be symptom-free of the ailment itself, even if just temporarily, is considered healthy even if the drug itself brings about numerous other side effects to the patient's overall health.

Government policy, medical schools and the health care industry primarily share this vision of health as the absence of symptoms belonging to the primary disease.

It is evident that patients who have a broader definition of health or who are more aligned with the WHO perspective will be looking for treatments and health care that is broader in scope and reflects their attitude towards health.

If you see health as simply the absence of symptoms, then quick fixes that get rid of the symptoms without addressing the cause are just as good as treatments that get rid of the symptoms and do address the cause, giving you back your vitality.

If your goal is to get rid of symptoms, then palliative drug therapy becomes a valid choice, but if the patient is looking for real health, then a different process is needed.

Most of North America defines health as an absence of symptoms. So long as there are painkillers, we kill the pain ? whether it be emotional or physical. Many patients have learned to accept that "covering it up" is good enough, or that it is all that is available.

In fact, the health care system we have created today is based on the "symptom-free" definition of health. So the goal is to get rid of the symptoms. The immediate result of getting rid of symptoms may be the ability to function, but functioning is not health from every perspective.

Let's take as an example, the sale of over-the-counter drugs for headaches. You may get rid of the symptoms, but you are still a person with headaches or prone to headaches. Big Pharma has an inherently advantageous rationale to see drugs as the solution for health. There are many followers of that vision.

As cited on Chiro One Wellness Center's website (www. chiroone.net), "In the United States alone, 50 million people have frequent headaches that result in 157 million lost work days, $50 billion in health care expenses, and $10 million in visits to doctors' offices. Most headache sufferers turn to over-the-counter drugs as their only form of relief. Americans spend an estimated $4 billion annually on over-the-counter medications for treatment of headache pain, often providing only temporary relief and causing a variety of unpleasant side effects."

In Canada, according to Headache Network Canada, "More than 3 million women in Canada suffer from migraines, and 92% of them miss work, school or family functions as a result. Those who suffer frequent attacks lose an average of seven workweeks a year. Migraines alone cost the Canadian economy about $500 million a year."

We have a medical economy driven by a quick fix, profit-hungry industry. Accordingly, the patients seeking our help will fall within a spectrum of "gullible consumers" and skeptics.

As doctors, do we have a role in expanding the expectations of what is considered health? Can we broaden patients' views on health, or are we technicians in the system, merely filling out prescriptions, enabling the desires of the "consumer" patients? Do commercial interests educate these desires? Is it our role to be educators in health care? How much are our prescriptions aligned with pharmaceutical interests?

Not everyone is comfortable with the industry's definition of health these days. The disillusioned and the skeptics are growing in numbers. What can we offer them? If they're not within our scope of practice, do we know where to refer them? Do we know where to find solutions that are compatible with their definition of health or experience of health?

The patient's relationship to their symptoms is the biggest factor in determining their informed objectives.

The spectrum ranges from perceiving symptoms as the body's enemy, to seeing them as signs that will help to refocus their lives and that are imbued with meaning and wisdom.

A more philosophical and spiritual perspective informs the relationship patients have to their symptoms. It's a perspective that's hard to capture in pill form. Even coronary heart disease can be either a prescription for heart and cholesterol medications, or a plan for exercise, healthy eating habits, lifestyle modifications and emotional investigations.

The Relationship to Symptoms

For most in the Western paradigm, the underlying assumption regarding symptoms is that SYMPTOMS ARE THE ENEMY. Symptoms are seen as the cause. They are not seen as an expression of the body; instead, the body is viewed as the victim of these manifestations.

Symptoms are seen as attacking and fighting against the body, driven by some outside force for which the body has little responsibility. The war on symptoms, or pain, resembles real war, where two factions are seen as separate and at odds, rather than as intrinsically interconnected and dependent on a greater consciousness and desire for real change. Possibly the same financial interests that keep wars alive are also the backbone keeping the "war" on our own body an accepted feature of the predominant culture.

We have already witnessed the incredible death tolls

that result when we oversimplify the debate about health to a choice between symptoms and no symptoms, pain and no pain. According to the 2003 medical report "Death by Medicine" by Drs. Gary Null, Carolyn Dean, Martin Feldman, Debora Rasio and Dorothy Smith, there are **783,936** deaths in the USA annually due to conventional medical mistakes. That's the equivalent of six jumbo jet crashes a day for an entire year!

These are iatrogenic deaths, that is to say, through the effects of drugs and errors of drugs, and not natural disease.

Basically, the definition of "health" — which is seen as a "war" against part of the body, has just a partially "functioning body" as its best outcome. That paradigm tends to look at symptoms as inconveniences that get in the way of daily activity. Thus the fastest way to remove their presence, regardless of further complications down the road, is seen as the best way.

Symptoms are viewed as an enemy to the body. So what removes them, triumphs.

There is no thought directed to why the symptoms actually appeared, or that something may actually be causing the body to create these symptoms in the first place. The common "pragmatic" approach is to cut or burn, bandage and forget, basically decontextualize the body from nature and meaning.

Take the common treatment for gallstones as an example. I have seen so many patients with a history of gallstones who have had their gallbladder (GB) removed. Removing the GB will definitely eliminate the stones and even the possibility of the body creating further gallstones, BUT does anybody actually wonder why the body created the stones in the first place?

Surely it is obvious that by removing the product, and in some cases, the container, we still may not have removed the Creator? The body is still programmed to create stones. The surgery has not removed the program. So the poor patient may be symptom-free, but healthy? Not a chance!

And have we all forgotten what the gallbladder does? Who is going to step in and deal with the bile once it's gone? So now we have a program running in the body that wants to create stones, and the beginning of an overtaxed digestive system. And does anyone ask what happens when the digestive system gets overtaxed?

Certainly there are ways of covering up those symptoms too, and you can start taking drugs for indigestion, fatigue, high blood pressure and atherosclerosis. There is a drug that will address some part of the plethora of symptoms, but there is no drug in this circumstance that will ever, ever, EVER bring about health.

Probably one of the most troubling uses of symptom cover-up is the use of chemotherapy. In fact, it is the whole approach to a patient with cancer. The patient is rarely asked why they think they may have cancer, or what they think may have caused it, or what environmental exposures or traumatic incidences they've experienced which may have tipped the balance. It is not even routine procedure to check on the anti-oxidants status of the body, their PH levels or their ability to fight free radicals.

They are not given a chance to reflect upon their experience in a constructive way nor asked what they have changed in their lives because of it. There is no interest shown in lifestyle, dietary or any other changes, although it has been suggested that a large percentage of patients with cancer are making dietary and lifestyle changes in their lives. The presumption is that the cancer will either be "cut out" or destroyed with chemotherapy. The patient then engages in the "war" against cancer.

But the reality behind the scenes is not comforting. The rates of success are slim, and the negative side effects enormous. The chemotherapeutic agents, some derived from pesticides, others ravaged from industry setbacks, are used to "kill" one cancer while, in some cases, replacing it with another - the most common one being leukemia.

Cure rates for cancer are measured by survival for five years, and despite the statistically significant outcomes, the clinical outcomes are insignificant. What is the value to a patient to live four to six weeks longer in a highly medicated state? Nevertheless, monies and "research into drug" treatment is by and large aimed at destroying the cancer with an agent that also wreaks havoc on the other cells of the body.

Therapies that offer an integrative approach to dealing with patients who have cancer, as well as therapies that help facilitate the ability of the body itself to overcome the cancer, are not funded and often completely sabotaged.

Cancer is Serious Business

A point in case is the unbelievable situation Dr. Stanislaw Burzynski faced for more than 30 years. His story is retold in the recent documentary, "Cancer is Serious Business." Why has the government been trying to imprison Dr. Burzynski, who has cured hundreds of cancer patients, many of whom are still in remission 10 years after treatment?

The director of this film, Eric Merola suspects that it is because when Burzynski's "Antineoplastons" therapies are approved for public use, it will allow a single scientist (Dr. Stanislaw Burzynski) to hold the exclusive license to manufacture and sell these medicines on the open market, leaving Big Pharma out of the game of profiting from the most effective, gene-targeted cancer treatment the world has ever seen.

Today, Dr. Burzynski is once again being sued by the State of Texas, so the recently released documentary about his work is now offered free to the public.

As well-known osteopath and alternative medicine advocate Dr. Joseph Mercola says, "If we put the FDA on the stand today, we can not only expose this abuse of power, but participate in the first time in history the general public will be responsible for forcing a medicine into FDA-approval and into the public's hands. (That's almost as exciting as discovering a cure for cancer)."

Pain as a Symptom

Taking another example, such as pain following an injury, our perception of the role and function of pain will determine how we experience the pain and what we want to do about it. The "objective" of the patient is informed by their ability to place their symptoms into a framework and context determined by their knowledge, philosophical view, spiritual understanding and critical-thinking abilities. The onus is on the doctor to inform or facilitate their process. It is absurd to act as though medicine exists in a vacuum, that it is not culturally, politically and philosophically-based.

One can also look at pain as a symptom that something is wrong, that there is a reason for the pain. If you take a painkiller, you do just that—kill the pain and let the cause fester. In my practice I see countless patients who take multiple medications. Often they've received shots of cortisone to remove the inflammatory reaction of the body to the injured area.

While we must address the inflammation that the body is producing, it is more important to find WHY it is producing inflammation. We must understand the CAUSE of the inflammation and address it, not just decrease the body's reaction to it.

I'd like to share with you a personal story about my holiday in October 2011. I had a subluxation of the right shoulder upon arriving in Paris. The pain tore into my right scapula and down my deltoid, and my muscles became more rigid and fibrous by the hour. I ended up getting the shoulder reduced back into place by a kinesiologist who happened to be the daughter of the host of the bed and breakfast.

The pain was excruciating, as I had not realized the dislocation until I looked into a mirror and noticed the drop in shoulder height 48 hours after the incident. I had some relief, and the muscles now could accept some soothing since the "cause" — the dislocation — had been addressed.

Traveling is never an optimal time for "rest," and I managed to dislocate it and get it reduced again, this time with an osteopathic doctor. I then went to the hospital to rule out any other problems and the X-ray showed no fracture, so they sent me home with painkillers and anti-inflammatories and told me to keep my arm in a sling for a few weeks.

I tried the painkillers, which gave some relief, albeit short-lived, but by the second day had no further effect. I took the anti-inflammatories but had too much nausea and discomfort and I had to stop them.
I was instructed to keep the arm completely still and to ice it.

The pain grew worse again, though it was clear that the shoulder was now in the proper position. I saw another osteopath a couple of times who explained how important it was to do passive motion with the arm so that I did not develop capsulitis. She suggested ice alternating with heat.

It was a strange experience being the patient as I was subjected to many different strategies and recommendations (hot/cold; motion/no motion). As there were some contradictions, I had to search for the "solution" most aligned to my belief system. There must also be timing and the right therapy which can join the dots and allow an old injury to be healed through the appearance of a new one.

It is at this point that I interjected with my personal experience as a doctor. I realized that my brain was holding on to the injury and not allowing the muscles to relax and assume their normal position. It took every effort to drop my curled-up "protection position" to a more relaxed position and benefit from the small range of motion I had (about 15 degrees in all directions).

As I sat in the waiting room, the doctor on call suggested I take Arnica and Rescue Remedy, as my body was "stuck." In fact, after I had taken the remedy, my whole body relaxed and I felt the trauma release. Not just this trauma, but an older one, as if my body had remembered an earlier memory.

To brace myself from a fall during gym class in my teens, my shoulder took a huge impact during the fall. Though the shoulder stayed intact, the trauma still lived in the tissues, and got reignited with this current accident. What was remarkable was that I felt a certain sense of relief; I guess "emotional" relief, but not much greater sense of range of motion.

After this session, I had 30 degrees of motion passively, and it became clear to me that I needed to keep the motion up. The holiday was almost over, and when I returned I became the patient at my own clinic. A colleague of mine treated me, and after one hour I had 180-degree active motion laterally, and only a slight tug on the insertion of the tendon of supraspinatus.

The treatment allowed my nervous system to reboot and recalibrate so that I was able to get past the trauma and memory of guarding and on with the healing. It is clear to me that drugs and physical therapy may have a place, but there must be a connection to the internal healing mechanism for efficient recovery to take place.

In contrast to this approach, cortisone shots just confuse the body. Cortisol is a compound the body actually creates and uses as part of its immune system, releasing it when the body is stressed. When we inject cortisone artificially, we are confusing the body's immune system through an outside "chemical force" which acts to suppress our body's own immune reactions.

This practice does not allow the immune system to start up and get in gear, but rather replaces its functioning. And we wonder why we have so many autoimmune diseases? Giving a cortisone shot also gives a confusing message to the patient. It creates a false sense of recovery, and therefore a false sense of security.

There must also be timing and the right therapy which

can join the dots and allow an old injury to be healed through the appearance of a new one

Since 1992 I cannot even start to count how many patients who received cortisone shots felt a decrease of pain and proceeded to take on activities which they would have otherwise been unable to do, and as a result "re-injured" themselves.

Call me crazy, but is it really a re-injury when you haven't yet dealt with the primary injury?

Because of that false sense of security, the patients went ahead and played golf and "snap," something went, starting the inflammation and pain up again. Only this time, because of the abuse of the joint not properly cared for (because its owner could no longer detect pain), the situation was significantly worsened.

And to top it off, for most patients who return to their doctors the cortisone shots have little suppressive effect long-term. In fact, the effect is often neutral by the third injection. The body gets used to the cortisone and develops a tolerance so that the doses necessary to continue the suppressive effect would literally kill the patient.

Now the joint has deteriorated, unbeknownst to the patient who does not FEEL the pain, and now there is more PAIN.

In the next section on "assessment," in which we review recent research on pain and the problems encountered with the definition of chronic pain, pain management issues and the paucity of treatment options, we see why it is crucial that the patient be an engaged agent in their healing journey.

What role do we, as doctors, have to play in the creation of disillusioned patients suffering in pain from our lack of fully disclosing the components involved in dealing with pain, and not just opting for the most convenient "solution" that for the most part is short-term and destructive?

Symptoms Without a Name

Probably one of the most troubling presentations is the patient who is experiencing signs and symptoms of illness and is seeking a label to explain their discomfort, but is turned away by medical experts who give the patient a clean bill of health.

The approach of symptom management under existing disease categories has its limitations, not only as a medical system, but in the injustice to a large number of patients who have signs and symptoms that do not fit into The Merck Manual of Diagnosis and Therapy disease categories. Chronic fatigue, fibromyalgia and the many undetected cases of Lyme Disease serve as examples.

The system of classifying diseases with their "appropriate" drug solutions is very limited, because the patient's symptomatology may not always package itself well under the existing labels, causing real conditions to either not be treated at all or be managed by drugs that are indicated to diminish or inhibit the symptoms.

It is often in these presentations that we witness the flagrant compartmentalization of the patient's body.

Each part that produces a symptom receives a prescription, but the overall state of the patient is barely improved. Nothing reaches the underlying why behind all the accumulation of symptoms, and nothing speaks to the patient as a whole.

I had a patient who came to see me with a "clean bill" of health. She had had blood work done, which appeared to be all normal. She even had a CT scan showing no abnormal findings. She was admitted to the hospital with pain and given morphine. She was also given drugs for her nausea and anti-pyrutic drugs for her chills and fever. When there were no findings, she was dismissed with drugs to abate the symptoms.

Still finding herself suffering from stomach pain, which radiated to her back and appeared concomitantly with periodic chills and heat, she asked me whether I had anything more to offer her. I suggested a stool analysis, because all of her symptoms started after what she believed to be food poisoning from a restaurant. I suspected parasites and gave her remedies to help her body rebalance its flora and environment to make it less hospitable and conducive for parasites.

Had I not suspected parasites, I do not think the approach would have been very different. After all, giving her tools to rebalance her flora and her digestion would create the best conditions for her body to start repairing itself. It surprises me that we keep looking at the outside for the solutions that are on the inside.

The doctor's ability to discern both the story and the observation of the patient will lead him/her to the ability to assess the next step to take.

I am sure you know personally people who have taken numerous antibiotics, anti-inflammatories, and then anti-depressives, or anxiolytics in an attempt to address their symptoms. Some work successfully, and others to no avail.

What if we took a slightly different approach and concluded: When the body produces Symptoms, LISTEN; it is trying to say something.

This is true of pain, inflammation, disease and symptoms that are non categorizable.

What if we took a more integrative approach and looked at the production of these symptoms beyond our present contemporary paradigm?

If we take pain, for example, the most prevalent and contemporary FIRST approaches to pain are:

1. **Analgesics**, which remove the body's capacity to "feel" the pain;
2. **Anti-inflammatories,** which remove the body's reaction to the injury, and therefore decrease the pain of the inflammation;

3. **Surgery**, which severs the nerve pathway and permanently removes the pain sensation, and often the functioning of the part;
4. **Psychological therapies**, which help the patient deal with the pain;
5. **Tolerance of pain**, probably the saddest trend of all.

So many patients have experienced pain for such a long time that they've come to view it as normal or the way it's meant to be for them. Pain is NOT normal.

It is worth exploring other avenues outside of contemporary medicine. After all, what would you do if you had pain and your scope of medicine did not offer solutions? Would you really assume that there is nothing out there? Or would you attempt to get familiar with approaches that at least have case-by-case results?

And this is where Dr. Google lends a hand, and also acts as an endless indiscriminate source of options and perspectives, which can be overwhelming.

In my upcoming book and Radio Show Synergy Dialogues on Health, I explore the choices available to patients and what perspectives they offer on healing. It is important to know where we thrive and where we fail and never lose touch with our calling to help our patients seek solutions for their health.

American psychologist Ross Buck describes the qualities of a doctor as one who inspires in the patient a confidence in the patient's own ability to heal. To be effective, the patient-doctor relationship is paramount. The doctor has to listen, the patient has to develop trust and the doctor has to use her/ his own intuition.

According to Dr. Gabor Maté, "These are the qualities doctors seem to have lost as we have come to rely almost exclusively on 'objective' measures, technology-based diagnostic methods and 'scientific' cures."

Chapter Three

Assessment Part One

The Case for the Cause

"In healing, every bit of information, every piece of the truth, may be crucial. If a link exists between emotions and physiology, not to inform people of it will deprive them of a powerful tool."
Gabor Mate

At this point, we have now collected the subjective and objective symptoms of the patient and we need to make an "assessment" on their status.

Assessment is crucial as it determines the Plan. This is the place and time in which to evaluate and make sense of the entire symptomatology.

Our method(s) of evaluating will determine our action plan, thus understanding this phase is vital. Making a diagnosis is a significant part of our medical training, and, depending on the tradition, involves using the criteria in the Merck Manual of Diagnosis and Therapy (known as "The Merck Manual") as in "Western" conventional medicine, as well as "Eastern" alternative systems, such as Traditional Chinese Medicine ("TCM"), which looks at the pulse and tongue to gain clues to a condition, as well as homeopathic assessments, functional, muscular and skeletal systems, and nutritional and lifestyle components.

As a naturopathic doctor, many people are referred to me by their general practitioner (GP) or specialist. Often an individual will come on their own accord, having received an "assessment" from numerous other health care providers. My practice has uniquely positioned me to study and extrapolate an understanding of the various aspects that come into play when assessing a patient's symptoms.

Symptoms are usually what motivate a patient to see a doctor for diagnosis and treatment. Symptoms are the natural way a body expresses a state of dis-ease. Symptoms can be expressed emotionally or through physical pain as a body process.

Symptoms as they Manifest in the Body

Let's explore symptoms as they manifest in the body. Early on, symptoms often appear to be inflammatory or eliminatory in nature. This is the body's attempt to reach homeostasis, by trying to eliminate the problem and the body's waste products naturally. In the language of the "natural" industry, this process is often called "detoxification". Elimination takes place through the urine, skin, bowel, or lungs and ciliary glands.

Symptoms such as headaches, constipation, water retention and the many symptoms associated with liver dysfunction, such as hormonal imbalances, irritability, and gastro-enteric symptoms, often result from the body's inability to adequately perform these eliminatory functions.

Other symptoms, such as fever and inflammation,

involve the immune system's attempt to deal with a temporary imbalance of organisms, be they bacterial, fungal or viral.

The reason it is so important in the assessment to understand the symptoms the body is producing is because it gives us options in their management. If the symptoms are a product of the natural elimination process, these symptoms are to be regarded very differently than when they appear to be part of the symptomatology of a disease state.

Even faced with acute inflammatory or eliminatory symptoms, there are different treatment approaches. To put it simplistically, but somewhat accurately we have the choice: 1) to support the body in its process by assisting the organs and pathways the body has already engaged, or 2) to "attack" the offender believed to be the source of the disruption.

Ultimately, our assessment is based upon premises that are interpretations of biology, chemistry and physics, and as history has shown can become outdated and inaccurate in the face of new evidence or theories. Thus our "plan" is only as good as our assessment.

Germs vs. Disease: History and Perspective

The "attack" route, made popular by French chemist Louis Pasteur (1822-1895) and his "Germ Theory of Disease" is based on the notion that bacteria cause disease, and thus eliminating the bacteria would rid a patient of the pathology. This approach of ridding the body of the offending element seemed to make "scientific" sense at its onset and was embraced by allopathic Western medicine and microbiology in late 19th century Europe. However, it was refuted by a prominent physician and scientist with degrees in biology, physics, pharmacy and chemistry, Antoine Bechamp, in the face of the evolving research and the technology to evaluate the symptoms.

Despite scientific evidence disproving the Germ Theory of Disease, traditional Western medicine still teaches and practices the doctrine, claiming that fixed species of microbes invade the body and are the first cause of infectious disease. This concept, known as monomorphism (one-form), in which specific, unchanging types of bacteria cause specific diseases, forms the foundation of allopathic Western medicine. Thus, the need to find specific agents to counter the "attack."

The researches of Antoine Bechamp demonstrated that in fact it was the sick "terrain" of the person that attracted the bacteria and not the other way around. While it was formerly impossible to tell whether micro-organisms on dead tissue were a result of the disease or caused the disease, the Rife microscope allowed live cells to be viewed, which clearly established that germs (micro-organisms) are the result of disease (scavengers of dead cells) rather than the cause thereof. Germs were found to arise as primary symptoms of a general condition, rather than the cause.

It became clear that the surrounding environment (often referred to as the "terrain") and extracellular fluid attracted the conditions for the apparition of micro-organisms, which would then evolve into different forms as a response to their environment.

In light of these findings, even Pasteur believed that germs and bacteria are not the exact and primary cause of disease, but that the disease came first, the germ second. He stated, "The presence in the body of a pathogenic agent is not necessarily synonymous with infectious disease." Pasteur was aware that fermentation (which he studied extensively while formulating his germ theory and based on the previous work of Bechamp) only occurs in injured, bruised or dead material, and that bacteria are a natural result of fermentation, not the cause.

He realized later that germs and bacteria change their form in response to their environment. This concept was based on the original work of Bechamp, the originator of "pleomorphism"—where one organism can rapidly assume many forms and may exist in several stages at once—which also was demonstrated with the advent of the powerful Rife Universal Microscope, developed in the late 1930s and early 1940s.

Unfortunately, the basic presumptions for modern-day medicine were already in place, and Pasteur could not reverse the tide. It would seem that there were interests in the "solutions" which would profit industry, rather than place the onus of responsibility on the person's lifestyle, nutrition and environment. Bechamp was a big advocate of the importance of looking after oneself and self-responsibility.

The implication of Bechamp's discovery is that if the bacteria are not the cause, then what sets off the terrain in order to attract the bacteria that show up after? And what are the bacteria doing, if they are not the cause?

A healthy terrain is maintained by proper levels of nutrients, adequate oxygenation, the right electro-magnetic charge (i.e. a healthy cell carries an electromagnetic negative charge) and a proper acid/ alkaline balance. When we are "acidic" it is as if our body is starting the decay process. This is the prime attraction for yeast and fungus growth. Bacteria come on the scene to help clean up the debris that has been created as the byproducts of these micro-organisms. The more acidic the terrain, the harder it is for oxygen to enter and the more beneficial the environment is for anaerobic bacteria. It is a vicious cycle.

Yeasts, Fungus and Mold

Yeasts, fungus and mold produce disruptive waste products, which are found in the tissues of a person with a compromised terrain. Examples of the byproducts are acetaldehyde, oxalic acid, lactic acid, uric acid, and alcohol. In response to these metabolites, the liver produces low-density lipoprotein in order to bind the toxins. These new compounds have a tendency to become oxidized and stick to lesions in the artery. If these compounds bind to the walls of red blood cells, the circulation in the capillaries is compromised, and oxygen starvation and deprivation occurs in the tissues.

The amount of uric acid and acetaldehyde produced by yeast and fungus can be overwhelming to the body. Acetaldehyde is converted into alcohol in the liver and depletes its stores of magnesium, sulfur, hydrogen, and potassium as well as destroying essential enzymes. The body chelates uric acid and other toxins with fats, raising LDL cholesterol and neutralises it by binding minerals such as potassium, magnesium, sodium, zinc, and calcium to it. The immune system is provoked into trying to neutralize this process and to retard the yeast and fungus by releasing large amounts of free radicals.

Eventually, the cell may be converted entirely from normal fermentative metabolism (oxidative metabolism) to abnormal fermentative metabolism (absence of oxygen.)

"All fermentative cells and their acids carry an electromagnetic positive charge. These rotting cells and their acids act like glue, which causes healthy cells to attract and stick together. This leads to oxygen deprivation and the disturbance and disorganization of more healthy cells. Simply put, healthy cells begin to rot!....In all cancer autopsies lactic acid or yeast, fungus and mold is found, and sometimes both."

"Perhaps the connection is not being made. But medical science is beginning at least to notice, if not recognize the significance of, the presence of lactic acid and yeast in cancer. They are present in cancer, but are also present in the blood before cancer, and without the presence of other symptoms for that matter!

"Hopefully biologists will approach the question of why and how the yeast gets into someone's blood in the first place, rather than merely pursuing expensive DNA research to see if they can kill it. This is the mental limitation imposed by the germ theory—spend millions to kill a symptom of dietary and nutritional misguidance, without realizing that the human organism itself is the main source of the yeast." (source: www.laleva.org)

The toxins (acids) from the whole spectrum of these microforms combine to produce symptoms, or provoke the body to produce them. This toxic output of yeast, fungus and mold shows up as signs and symptoms of disruption in the body, but that is not to say that it is the microforms themselves that initiated the disease. They only show up because of a compromised biological terrain. Wainwright states: "If only medical science would take the trouble to look, scientists will observe the concept of pleomorphism. Once this cycle of development has begun, the terrain is further compromised, and a vicious circle of imbalance results." (Wainwright, 1997)

In the 1979 edition of Clinical Interpretation of Laboratory Tests, Frances K. Widmann, M.D., associate professor of Pathology at Duke University said, "The war between microorganisms (germ and viruses) continues unremittingly. 'Wonder drugs' have not eradicated infectious disease; they have merely changed the conditions and natural history of many infections. Organisms (microbes) display a remarkable capacity to adapt, so that drugs effective today become ineffective against the same type of infection tomorrow.

"Isn't it strange that modern scientists have become so deeply entrenched in the microbial infection theory of disease causation that they are unable to comprehend that infection is not infection ... but inflammation. Few people will consider chronic poisoning and/or malnutrition as possible factors in the futile search for disease eradication."

In an interesting study just published in June 2014, it was discovered that stress, emotional shock, or overexertion could indeed "biologically" create heart attacks or stroke.

The mechanism appears to be that when the body produces catecholamine hormones (a physiological stress response,) the normally existing bio floras on the arterial walls undergo dispersion and release enzymes that digest the arterial wall allowing plaque to rupture into the bloodstream.

The conclusion however is interesting.

"This research suggests that bacteria should be considered to be part of the overall pathology of atherosclerosis and management of bacteria within an arterial plaque lesion may be as important as managing cholesterol."

It is interesting that just like the idea that cholesterol is the culprit when it is well established now, that cholesterol is in fact the body's protective mechanism for arteries that have been ravaged by the effects of free radical damage. We are full of bacteria, it seems strange to me that the solution would be found in the bacteria. It does not seem to me that the bacteria are the cause of the heart attacks any more than the cholesterol. Both appear to be present in the cascade but should the solution not be found looking at other parameters? How can we decrease the effect of stress after the initial reaction has taken place? What makes stress so deadly in certain people? Since we all have bacteria, bacteria alone cannot be the solution. What other factors should we be taking into consideration?

How I Avoided a Hysterectomy

I was faced with these conflicting views toward disease and its ensuing treatment. In 2001, after refusing the hysterectomy recommended by my doctors at an Ontario Oncology ward to treat my Stage 4 cancer, I was dismissed from the hospital. Both the nurse and I, were in shock.

I can recall the head nurse towering over me with reproaches for what she perceived to be an irresponsible choice. "You have three kids! How could you risk your life like this?" she said. "Who will be around when you are gone? It is only your uterus, we are saving your life," she blurted out in disbelief. My shock, on the other hand, was not focused on my uterus either; I was concerned that if I had cancer, then

I had to get to the bottom of it. I had to remove the chances for the cancer to come back. Just cutting parts out would not be profound enough a therapy. I had to ensure that my own body was able to rid itself of this manifestation. I believed that otherwise, it would just come back.

After an awkward silence, the nurse let me know that if I was not going to accept the protocol suggested, I would also loose my opportunity to be monitored. For one moment, I could not understand how all this was connected. "Do you mean," I enquired, "that I cannot get monitored while I consider other options?" The release papers were presented. I signed. It was a scary few months as I had counted on the ability and the freedom of choice to get monitored and had not realized that the "freedom" came with strings attached.

Subsequently, to my great relief; I found a gynecologist and oncologist, trained with a wider view and perspective on how the body heals and what it requires to do so.

She was willing to monitor me and distinguish between an inflammatory and a fixed morbid state. Because I was being monitored I was able to support my body in re-establishing homeostasis and could monitor the inflammatory response advantageously and help my body re-establish an environment that was more conducive to health. I am (thankfully) still around.

The anti-invader approach (i.e. finding and eradicating the offending element) is also met with resistance from the body. When used as a short-term and infrequent strategy, this approach may be somewhat effective, but continually attempting to rid the body of invaders through the use of antibiotics and wonder drugs causes the body to mount its own resistance.

And herein lays a more philosophical question: are we really in a world in which "superbugs" are out to eradicate the human race? Or are we really in a world in which we need to learn how to manage and live alongside stressors, even if we believe them to be bacteria instead of our own body's lack of homeostasis? I tend to think it is the latter. If it were the former, then at the first sign of a cold everyone would get it as the bug would be imbued with such power as to take over our immune system and make us sick. Instead, what we commonly observe is that some of us get sick and some of us don't.

So it can't lie with the bug, but rather how "accommodating" we are to that bug. Surely, people know this on the inside, as often they will say, "I am so run down, I hope I don't get sick." What they are aware of is that their inner environment is just not up to par, not strong enough.

The advent of more antibiotic-resistant strains and the limited success of antifungal and antiviral treatments further refute the invader theory. Thus we are called to find other solutions based on how to best assist the body in managing these elements. We will address this point in depth in the following section.

When drawing conclusions about what course of action to prescribe, based on our understanding and assessment of the presenting symptoms, and whatever internal biological situation is in place, we must address the patient as a whole.

Emotions as a Symptom

Given that at least one-tenth of the North American population is taking some form of anti-psychotic medication, what we perceive to be the role of emotions in our health cannot be understated. Let's explore how people experience and what they tend to do with "emotions."

Interestingly, varying trends are developing alongside each other today, not the least of which is influenced by "Big Pharma" sales as part of the greater consumer society, who have been led to believe that the answers come from without and that happiness in life is attainable if only one takes this or buys that. Even the self-empowerment industry marvels at the "wanna-be," not the inner state of gratitude for who we are and what we already have.

The question really boils down to: Do we treat uncomfortable emotional states with drugs so that we are less aware of them, or do we get to the root and find out their role as "symptoms" of our whole being? Do we see our emotions in part as adaptive behaviours to unconscious programming, or "acute" responses to situations, which we need to look at more closely? The point is that we "produce" them; they are part of our symptomatology and are as relevant as our physical pain and other signs and symptoms.

If we look at the initial reaction to a feeling, we experience an emotion. There are three ways in which people commonly deal with their emotions — at least, the emotions that they have been made aware of — that they are conscious of.

They either:

1. **Suppress**. Keep the emotion in and deal with it internally.
2. **Express**. Expressing, in general, is seen as a positive step in our culture, whereas repressing is seen as negative, and in some cases "disease-causing."
3. **Release**. The approach is to "Release" a kind of letting go without attachment.

In contrast to the pharmacological industry, this approach does in effect promote personal responsibility and commitment to acknowledge and deal with one's pain and difficult emotions.

Methods intended for "emotion management" (Sedona, Levenson, Craine) and increasing references to this in the professional literature suggest that "expressing" has its limitations because the mind, through repetitions, re-creates the neuronal synapses that reinforce the unconscious attachment to the emotions. This is the main tenet of neurolinguistic programming (NLP) and any type of "brain-retraining" therapies. Repetitive expression reinforces these pathways and imprints the experience into our unconscious.

Many of the therapies based on constant expression

are of long duration, and rather than freeing one of the experiences, such therapy further justifies and reinforces the emotional reaction to the traumatic experiences.

In this light, "releasing," which represents a form of non-attachment, is a letting-go of the issue that has stirred the emotional reaction and eliminated its hold.

An example of this would be the transition from a state of anger to one of acceptance. As renowned therapist Byron Katie would say, a state in which one stops fighting with reality, a state in which one stops seeing the world in "shoulds" or "should nots." Reality is what it is, and we are much more productive when we do not fight with "what is."

Much energy is wasted in "reaction," fighting against what is; very little positive outcome can be expected in such a struggle. The phase of positive acceptance of a situation is usually the phase that allows for positive action.

One predominant presumption found in many schools of psychology, that one can in fact "suppress" emotions and that this suppression leads to illness, is unsupported by science. If we take for example a person who is experiencing a state of overwhelm, the right brain will manifest this state. If the right brain is overwhelmed, the left-brain may signal to it to stop forwarding information for immediate action by the left side of the brain.

However, this is not suppression; it is the body's best attempt at coping with being overwhelmed. The ensuing desensitizing or detachment is in its own right a symptom. It is the expression of an over-driven left-brain coping to the best of its ability. Terminology is important—in fact, the emotions are not suppressed, they are just expressed in another way. The body will find a way to manifest them. So if we don't separate the mind from the body, any state of illness, including emotional ones, will not be suppressed, just expressed in another way.

The Body Cannot Suppress Itself

The body is not in any way equipped to suppress itself. Illness is either expressed through signs and symptoms or released through elimination or detoxification pathways. There is no covert activity that self-sabotages itself. The body is either expressing symptoms of detoxification and ridding itself of debris from the environment or from its own metabolism, or it is reacting with an inflammatory process in an attempt to gain homeostasis.

An "unexpressed" symptom is not a suppressed symptom. An unexpressed symptom could be a family disposition for asthma or cardiovascular disease, which has not yet, and perhaps never will, manifest itself (i.e. it's in a "dormant" state.)

It is really a mental construct to believe that one can suppress one's emotions consciously. One either has them or does not. Short-term management strategies for dealing with emotions that do not fit into the social construct of society exist, and people make conscious choices not to "share" their emotions, but to call that "suppression" has other implications.

Short-term strategies can include avoidance through distraction, social isolation, or introspective behaviours, but eventually an emotion is either naturally released with no further ramifications or is still being experienced, whether it is expressed or not. From the perspective of homeopathic medicine it is a symptom, and it informs the treatment choice.

I am not convinced that an "expressed" emotion is any different than a felt and "unexpressed" emotion on the face of it. What might make the difference between the two is how one processes the emotion itself, either alone or with another. The processing of emotion, which occurs when people "retreat" into themselves, may well be part of the healing response, much as "sickness behaviour" is part of the immune system's repertoire for dealing with stress.

More to the point, what might be making all the difference is how our bodies interpret emotional information. Dr. Gabor Mate, a Canadian physician who specializes in the study and treatment of addiction, presents numerous case studies in which early childhood experiences which elicited strong emotions in the young person were stored and formed the basis for interpretations of future events. Science explains this process through the actions of the hippocampus, as discussed later in this section. The question is not whether emotions affect the body, it is rather what we make of this information therapeutically.

That emotions can be consciously suppressed is purely a theory. The theory would lead us to believe that emotions are suppressed in the unconscious from the conscience in a conscious way. As practitioners, we are either trying to help people process by providing them with methods they can use to address "conscious is-sues", or we are totally focused on methods that liberate unconsciously held patterns of belief that have created their own patterns. Either way, the body responds to our thoughts and emotions. (Several therapeutic approaches such as the Emotional Freedom Technique, Psych-K, and hypnotherapy to name a few also deal with "un-conscious" patterns of belief as a way to address our emotions.)

Dulling the Senses

The only way to interfere with this natural process is if the person can be sufficiently drugged not to feel their emotion. This is suppression. It is a conscious choice (maybe ill-informed) to suppress the emotions, whether expressed or internalized.

If we observe the major trends seen in psychiatric medicine, then the "medical intervention" is ultimately based on keeping the patient's feelings out of their reach by dulling the senses in one way or another. The approach is to introduce a drug action to suppress the emotion. This can only be done by through an external drug effect; the body cannot do this on its own.

The point here is that the body cannot consciously suppress its own emotions, but requires outside intervention to suppress what the body cannot do by itself. The "health" validity of such an approach makes no logical sense, as we know that "consciously" driving emotions out of our reach does not give us any possibility to address their cause or get to the source of their appearance.

I do not think that the human body was designed with the capacity to consciously suppress anything. In fact, I believe that "suppression" is an artificial construct, which nonetheless still guides Cartesian-based contemporary medicine.

If we approach the patient as a whole, there is always an expression of the emotion—what affects the emotions may well be manifested in the tissues. The point is that it is expressed somewhere if we stop taking such a compartementalized view of the human body/person.

Psychiatric Medicine: A Bit of History

The history of psychiatric medicine is a case in point. Starting with 125 psychiatric diagnoses, and a very small percentage of people who fit the criteria set by the profession at the time, the main goal was patient management. Because internment in wards was the predominant treatment approach, the drugs used were primarily forms of sedatives that affected the frontal lobes of the brain, making patients docile and easier to manage. The thought of curing a patient's mental state was not even part of the goal. With the advent of Miltown, it was discovered that there was indeed a market for helping people dissociate from their feelings and emotions.

The development of the psychiatric drug industry at the time based itself on a theory that had no science to substantiate it. The hypothesis was that there existed a chemical imbalance in the brain that produced sets of symptoms. The industry took advantage of the creation of many categories of disease that required psychotic drugs to alleviate, but neither the actual scientific basis of the drug action nor the chemical imbalances were understood. These categories were conjured up by grouping sets of symptoms in order to create "disease categories." It is only recently, with the advent of the field of psychoneuroimmunology, that some understanding of the interaction of emotions and biochemistry is being developed.

It is interesting to note that both the Diagnostic and Statistical Manual of Mental Disorders (DSM-I) and DSM-II, published by the American Psychiatric Association and used to provide a common language and standard criteria for the classification of mental disorders, differed from the DSM-III and later editions in that DSM-III took a brain-based approach. Instead of describing possible psychological causes for mental distress, it simply provides clinicians with symptoms that fit categories. However, these categories were almost broad enough to apply to anyone, at any time in life. "With no science to back it up, these newly proposed disorders and the checklist that went with them were subject to intense negotiations, compromises, alterations and heated debates" according to Drs. David Shaffer and Julian Whitaker, both mental health practitioners.

The industry boomed, and sales of the antidepressant Miltown, marketed to busy moms, white-collar office workers and pregnant women to alleviate "stress," to $80 billion dollars a year.

The DSM-IV lists 374 separate mental disorders, each with its own name and definition. The trend has definitely been to create categories of "diseases" based on a contrived set of symptoms for which drug therapies could be prescribed. What is even more telling is that the mainstream psychiatric community are developing even more categories by declaring certain behaviours as "abnormal" or "unnecessary." An example is the category "bereavement"; it's considered abnormal if prolonged beyond 6 weeks. The new DSM-V, published in 2013 has even more issues in that the scientific basis of the categories are being questioned. The director of the National Institutes of Mental Health has announced that the federal agency–which provides grants for research on mental illness–will be "re-orienting its research away from DSM categories." Thomas Insel's statement came just weeks before the scheduled publication of the DSM-V, the fifth edition of the Diagnostic and Statistical Manual. Insel writes:

"While DSM has been described as a 'Bible' for the field, it is, at best, a dictionary, creating a set of labels and defining each. The strength of each of the editions of DSM has been 'reliability'–each edition has ensured that clinicians use the same terms in the same ways. The weakness is its lack of validity. Unlike our definitions of ischemic heart disease, lymphoma, or AIDS, the DSM diagnoses are based on a consensus about clusters of clinical symptoms, not any objective laboratory measure." The DSM will be replaced with the "research Domain Criteria," which will be based on neural, genetic and cognitive data. The only caveat worth noting here is that Insel himself states: "we cannot design a system based on biomarkers or cognitive performance because we lack the data." The net result is that we go from nebulous to non-existent. What is equally shocking is that in a 2009 Point/Counterpoint article, Lisa Cosgrove, PhD and

Harold J. Bursztajn, MD noted that "the fact that 70% of the task force members have reported direct industry ties---an increase of almost 14% over the percentage of DSM-IV task force members who had industry ties--- shows that disclosure policies alone, especially those that rely on an honor system, are not enough and that more specific safeguards are needed."

Depression Screening

Returning to the therapeutic effects on patients, evolutionary psychologist Paul Andrews, an assistant professor in the Department of Psychology, Neuroscience & Behaviour, is the lead author of a recent article in the journal Frontiers of Psychology (2011). He analyzes the common practices in psychiatry and concludes that patients who have used antidepressant medications can be nearly twice as susceptible to future episodes of major depression. Meta-analysis suggests that people who have not taken any medication are at a 25% risk of relapse, compared to 42% or higher for those who have taken and gone off an antidepressant.

Similar research conducted under the "TeenScreen" Program conducted in the USA claims that identifying and treating "at risk" children can prevent suicide. Dr. David Healy and Graham Aldred, from the Department of Psychological Medicine, Cardiff University, reviewed published SSRI antidepressant reports and found quite the opposite. They found to the contrary, that there was an increase in suicide risk.

Depression screening in the general community

accounts for 60 million prescriptions for antidepressants written in the U.S. That's 10% of the population, including 1.5 million children." (Glenmullen, 2000) It should come to no surprise that these surveys were funded by pharmaceutical companies. (Pringle, 2006)

My clinical experience reflects these findings. Doctors too readily prescribe anti-depressants, which in their own right produce a cascade of symptoms that put the adult, or child, in a worse predicament. This is further exacerbated by the difficult and emotionally disturbing withdrawal symptoms so many experience if they decide to choose a drug-free route.

Even without taking into consideration that the criteria and circumstances for the patients who did not take medication were not considered, other than that they did not ingest the said antipsychotic drugs, and aside from post treatment "relapse" conveniently fitting the criteria for depression as laid out by the DSM-IV, Andrews raises great concern as to the lack of benefit of these drugs, especially regarding their harmful effects.

How Depression Bounces Back

Anti-depressants interfere with the brain's natural self-regulation of serotonin and other neurotransmitters, Andrews explains, and the brain can overcorrect once medication is suspended, triggering new depression. All forms of antidepressants disturb the brain's natural regulatory mechanisms. "We found that the more these drugs affect serotonin and other neurotransmitters in your brain — and that's what they're supposed to do — the greater your risk of relapse once you stop taking them," Andrews says. "All these drugs do reduce symptoms, probably to some degree, in the short-term. The trick is what happens in the long-term?

"Our results suggest that when you try to go off the drugs, depression will bounce back. This can leave people stuck in a cycle where they need to keep taking antidepressants to prevent a return of symptoms". (Neale et al., 2011) The authors looked at studies of four types of antidepressants: MAOI (monoamine oxidase inhibitor), SSRI (selective serotonin reuptake inhibitors), SNRI (serotonin and norepinephrine reuptake inhibitors), and TCA (tricyclics).

Each of these drugs affects at least one of the major neurotransmitters: serotonin, norepinephrine, or dopamine. In this particular research, symptom suppression (i.e. what these drugs are designed to do) is found not only to be ineffective long-term but also detrimental to the brain's own regulatory system. "There's a lot of debate about whether or not depression is truly a disorder, as most clinicians and the majority of the psychiatric establishment believe, or whether it's an evolved adaptation that does something useful," says Paul Andrews. (Nauert, Rick, 2011)

Furthermore, with the recent work of Dr. Daniel Amen, who has performed functional studies of tens of thousands of brains, the brain is actually being studied as an organ in its own right. Many "mood disorders" can actually be visualized as distortions and concavities in the actual brain and can be readily repaired with proper nutrition and "brain food".

To conclude, in order to assess a patient's presenting symptomatology it becomes of fundamental importance to establish what your framework or approach will be. Do you see the expression of their symptoms as a DSM "disease category," or as the body's cry for help? Will you categorize their symptomatology into "disease entities," which will require prescriptions either on the biological level, as in antibiotics, anti-inflammatories, or emotional, as in antipsychotics?

Do you fundamentally believe that the body is at war with the environment and is being invaded, or that it's in a self-destroying war with itself? Or do you believe that you are witnessing a body in need of nutritional support, emotional support, environmental support, or maybe just a treatment that can hone in on the body's self-healing capacity?

And very fundamentally, behind that is the question whom are we treating—a patient with a set of symptoms which we call a disease, or a disease which happens to be in that patient?

The next two sections on pain and psychoneuro-immunology (PNI), the study of the mind-body connection, will highlight the limitations of the Cartesian approach to disease as separate from the patient and the arbitrary and unfounded separation of the body from the mind. As Plato said, "The part can never be well unless the whole is well." We will explore different scientific findings that will help you answer those questions for yourself.

Assessment Part Two

From Story to Metaphor

Assessing a patient's health requires us to consider the cause of their symptoms. Conducting a full history of the circumstances and the physical and emotional environment that surrounded the onset of a patient's condition provides information needed to determine the root cause of the symptoms and make an accurate health assessment.

Understanding the factors which may have contributed to a patient's illness can help us address and eliminate the cause, rather than merely alleviate the symptoms of a condition. The fact that the mind and body work as one, with our physical and emotional reactions intricately intertwined and affecting our neuro-immune pathways, makes it imperative for us to expand our approach to both assessment and prescription.

Mind Body Spirit: History and Perspective

The earliest physicians understood that health encompassed the mind, body and spirit, beginning in the 2nd century with Claudius Galen, an influential Roman physician, who noticed that any part of the body can affect any other part through neural connections, thus establishing the beginning precepts of psychoneuroimmunology.

This relationship between emotional and physical health has been explored and confirmed throughout history, often in contrast to dominant medical practice and philosophy. In one of Plato's dialogues, Socrates quotes the Thracian doctor Hippocrates' criticism of his Greek colleagues, "This is the reason why the cure of so many diseases is unknown to the physicians of Hellas; they are ignorant of the whole. For this is the great error of our day in treatment of the human body, that physicians separate the mind from the body." (Mate, 2011 p.9)

In the 1800s, French physiologist Claude Bernard coined the concept of the extra-cellular fluid as the "milieu interieur," literally "the environment within." Bernard postulated that changes in this internal state were the body's adaptive responses designed to maintain conditions indispensable to vital activity. "Sickness and death are only a dislocation or perturbation of that mechanism," wrote Bernard.

Likewise, 19th century French biology professor and researcher, Antoine Bechamp, whom we discussed earlier, talked of the "terrain of the body" and noted the importance of caring for oneself to prevent disease. An advocate of a healthy lifestyle, including wholesome nutrition, a healthy environment, and hygienic cleanliness, Bechamp believed that people do not catch diseases, but in fact create them with what they eat, drink, think and feel. "If we create an unhealthy body, then the crew of scavengers, such as microbes, viruses, and parasites— what we refer to as "germs"—come in to clean up the debris."

In the early 1800's Samuel Hahnemann, known as the Father of Homeopathy, viewed disease, including mental illness, as a dis-attunement of the "vital principle"—that which animates all living matter. He saw symptoms as an expression of a derangement in the homeostatic balance of the body and was one of the first physicians to explore the importance of hygiene and treat mentally ill patients with homeopathy, in contrast to popular treatments for mental conditions in his day, such as beatings and bloodlettings to remove evil spirits.

In his collected works and the Organon of Medicine, Hahnemann created and expounded homeopathic medicine to help restore balance in patients with particular emphasis on those diagnosed with schizophrenia and delusionary states.

Hahnemann noted that finding the appropriate remedy involved taking into account the complete picture of the patient's lifestyle, including personality, temperament and emotional disposition, eating and sleeping habits, and all of the physical manifestations, the so-called "expression" of the disease.

In homeopathy, a patient's mental and emotional states must be understood in order to find the remedy for skin eruptions, asthma, gastritis and the like. The teaching more than two hundred years ago in Germany, where homeopathy was studied in medical school, was that there is never one remedy for a set condition, since the physician would always
have to take into account how the patient would experience the condition.

Take malaria for example. Hahnemann discovered that quinine produced intermittent fevers, very similar to what we observe with malaria. Thus quinine, seemingly capable of producing malaria symptoms in a healthy person, was used to cure malaria in those afflicted by it. This is demonstrated in Hahnemann's earliest research on Peruvian bark.

Today, quinine is used as a malaria prophylactic. The reason that it is not 100% effective is because quinine only produces symptoms typical of one expression of malaria. In homeopathic medicine, there are at least 50 expressions of the symptoms of malaria as witnessed by those afflicted. So if one went to see a homeopathic physician, one would not necessarily receive quinine, but would instead receive the remedy that best suits the current expression of this disease in the individual patient.

The Fight or Flight Response

As early as 1915, Harvard physiology professor Walter Cannon observed in his work with animals that emotions such as anxiety, distress, or rage, caused the stomach to stop moving (Cannon, 1915). His earlier findings regarding the effects of emotion and perception on the autonomic nervous system, namely the sympathetic and parasympathetic responses, introduced the concept of the "fight or flight" response and were published in The Mechanical Factors of Digestion, in 1911.

Likewise, in the early 1930's University of Montreal researcher Hans Selye demonstrated stress' effects on animals. Despite exposure to physical and mental stressors, animals adapted and healed. However, continued exposure to stressors eventually weakened the immune system, killing the animal. Enlargement of the adrenal gland, gastric ulcerations and atrophy of the thymus, spleen and other lymphoid tissue were physiological changes caused by stress. These studies further validated efforts to investigate the connection between emotional states affecting physiological behaviour and states.

Biology of Emotions

In 1975, scientists Robert Ader and Nicholas Cohen demonstrated classic conditioning of the immune function in their experiments with rats at the University of Rochester, in the process coining the term "psychoneuroimmunology." (Ader & Cohen, 1975) The experiment demonstrated that the nervous system—and even our thoughts—can influence the immune system. Scientists formerly believed that each physical system functioned independently.

Another breakthrough showing neuro-immune interactions occurred years later, in 1981 when Indiana University of Medicine scientist David Felten found nerves connected to blood vessels and cells of the immune system, as well as in the thymus and spleen ending at clusters of immune function-regulating lymphocytes, macrophages and mast cells.

Combining their research, Ader, Cohen and Felten edited Psychoneuroimmunology in 1981, proposing that the brain and immune system work together to keep the body healthy. Following suit, in 1985 neuropharmacologist Candace Pert at Georgetown University demonstrated that the cell walls and the brain have neuropeptide-specific receptors. (Pert et al.; Ruff et al. 1985) This research provided scientific proof that emotions and immunity are interrelated.

According to Steven Maier, Ph.D., the body can translate a blood-borne signal into a neural signal. Maier explained the importance and relevance of the vagus nerve in transmitting information to the brain. This nerve acts as an immunomodulator, regulating the production of pro-inflammatory cytokines.

Maier explains that the blood-brain barrier does not allow cytokines produced by the macrophages to cross. Instead, the vagus nerve translates the information for the brain.

Here's what happens: "your macrophage chews on a bacteria, it releases interleukin-1 into the neighboring space, the interleukin-1 binds to the receptor on the para-ganglia, which sends neurotransmitters to activate the vagus nerve, which sends a signal to the brain". This neural signal triggers the brain to make its own interleukin-1 and that sets off the sickness response and sends signals back to the immune system, further activating immune cells and continuing the feedback loop. Maier concludes by saying, "We have a complete, bidirectional immune-to-brain circuit." (Maier, 1993, p. 321-324)

So what does this really mean? We know that cytokine synthesis and release is an essential component of the immune system. We also understand that inappropriate and excessive production of cytokines results in a systemic inflammatory response which damages our organs. The vagus nerve, by means of neuro-immune communication in a pathway called the "cholinergic anti-inflammatory pathway," provides us with a fast, efficient and localized means of controlling the immune response and preventing excessive inflammation.

Communication With The Vagus Nerve

Does that mean we may be able to communicate to our vagus nerve and decrease inflammatory responses? It has been shown that acupuncture, relaxation therapy and biofeedback can evoke vagus nerve response. (Johnston, G.R. (2009, p.453-62)

The vagus nerve starts at the brain stem and connect to the stomach and lungs. I think everyone has experienced firsthand how perceived stress affects our stomach and respiratory system. It is hardly surprising then that the attitude and way in which we eat and breathe affects the health of our immune system.

What has been established is that emotions will trigger physiological changes in the body, which then, particularly through the neuro-hormonal circuits, trigger feedback loops to the brain. We also know that "stress" can be triggered emotionally, as well as by an infectious agent. The pathways the body uses to cope with the stressors are the same. Both infectious agents (noted in the body) and acute stressors (prompting our "fight or flight" reaction) engage neural, immune and hormonal pathways that respond quickly to achieve homeostasis.

Stress & Disease

Today, chronic diseases and "stress" are pandemic in our societies. It is a rare patient with a medical issue which is not compounded by multifaceted circumstances and reactions in the body. The body's processes affect the mind, and simultaneously the mind's processes affect the body, but through different pathways. Let's take a look at these pathways in more detail.

The two major pathways involved in this cross-talk are the hypothalamus-pituitary-adrenal (HPA) axis and the sympathetic nervous system (SNS).

The Sympathetic Nervous System

Neurotransmitters called peptides enable communication between the mind and the body through the sympathetic nervous system (SNS). The role of the sympathetic-adrenal-medullary (SAM) pathway is to activate the autonomic nervous system (ANS) using these neurotransmitters and neuropeptides for direct communication with immune cells. Three neurotransmitters—norepinephrine, serotonin, and dopamine—are essential for neural communication.

Neurotransmitters attach to immune cells and affect their ability to multiply or destroy cells. According to research by Freeman and Lawlis, it is likely that the emotions resulting from stressors may increase susceptibility to disease (because the brain releases neurotransmitters during times of stress.) (Freeman & Lawlis, 2001)

They further report that neuropeptides, secreted by the brain and immune system, have a crucial role in mind/body interactions since immune cells carry receptors for all the neuropeptides. Note that the limbic system, the part of the brain that regulates emotions, is particularly rich in receptor sites for neuropeptides. Thus, it is reasoned that neuropeptides are a significant factor involved in the effects of the mind on immunity. (Freeman & Lawlis, 2001) As mentioned prior, a June 2014 study explains in biological terms the direct effect of stress on heart attacks and strokes (.Lanter mBio, June 2014 DOI: 10.1128/mBio.01206-14)

Research has demonstrated that neurotransmitters that were once thought found only in the brain are also located in the immune system. Therefore, any immune function can occur in the brain or anywhere in the immune system. When the central nervous system (CNS) receives cognitive stimuli, it conveys that information through hormonal pathways to receptors on immune cells such as macrophages.

The neurotransmitters that are released from the brain during times of stress result in an increase in interleukin-1 in the hippocampus. "Stress and infection activate overlapping neural circuits that critically involve interleukin-1 as a mediator," explains Maier. (Azar, Beth, 2001, p.34)

The importance of this discovery is that not only does stress produce the expected "stress response," it also produces exactly the same behavioural changes, including decreased food and water intake and decreased exploration, and physiological changes, including fever, increased white blood cell count and activated macrophages, seen in the "sickness response."

This means that what we may perceive as emotional or psychological stress affects our body in the same way as if the body was experiencing stress from a physical or biological source. As Maier noted in his researches, "These animals are physically sick after stress. You see everything you see with infection."

Stress Management Pathway

The primary stress management pathway is the hypothalamic-pituitary-adrenal (HPA) axis that signals the endocrine system to release hormones. The HPA axis responds to physical and mental challenges to maintain homeostasis in part by controlling the body's cortisol level.

These hormones, particularly those produced by the thyroid and adrenals (cortisol), along with neurotransmitters and neuropeptides, directly affect the immune system and can increase or decrease cellular processes. Freeman and Lawlis found that certain hormones, such as cortisol and epinephrine, are released in higher amounts when an individual is under great stress. In addition, these hormones are known to depress T-cell activity, and thus one's immune system (Freeman & Lawlis, 2001)

The immune system helps to maintain physical homeostasis. Stress-induced alterations in the immune system occur primarily in the spleen, lymph nodes, and lymphoid tissues. However, there are numerous components of the immune system that may be modified by stress hormones.

Let's not forget that 70-80% of the immune system lies behind the gut and that cells communicates with each other via neurotransmitters, so that we really have a body-wide communication system.

Jacobs found that individuals who are under stress have an increased risk of developing autoimmune diseases. The most common stress-related autoimmune diseases are psoriasis, rheumatoid arthritis, and multiple sclerosis. (Jacobs, 2001, S83-S92)

The Body's Response to Stress

The limbic system (emotional motor system) is the primary area of the brain dealing with stress. The hypothalamus of the limbic system sends chemical and nerve signals to the pituitary gland, which then communicates with the adrenal glands that sit on top of the kidneys. Recall that perceived stress causes the limbic system to immediately respond via the autonomic nervous system, which consists of a complex network of endocrine glands that automatically regulate metabolism. When the sympathetic system dominates, we secrete hormones that cause inflammation. When we are relaxed, the parasympathetic system dominates and secrete acetylcholine which diminishes inflammation. Some of the signals sent through the HPA activate certain glands or organs and some of the signals inhibit or suppress certain glands or organs. This is the initial step of the stress response. There are two parallel pathways that emerge from the HPA, the epinephrine pathway and the cortisol pathway. In the face of perceived threat, the adrenal glands release adrenalin, otherwise known as epinephrine. If the threat is severe or prolonged, they release cortisol, which travels to the brain and remains there much longer than adrenalin.

Increased cortisol levels have immediate perceptible effects on the body such as weight gain. Normally, cortisol is secreted by the adrenal glands in a diurnal pattern, meaning that concentration in the bloodstream vary depending upon the time of day (normally, cortisol levels are highest in the early morning and lowest around midnight). When you are stressed, this pattern is altered. The natural rhythm of the body is disturbed and consequently can affect blood pressure regulation, carbohydrate and fat metabolism, insulin release and blood sugar regulation, as well as energy.

A less known effect of cortisol is its ability to divert blood glucose from the brain, in particular the hippocampus, to muscles. Cortisol impedes and compromises many functions in the brain, such as the ability of the hippocampus to create new memories.

A study by James McGaugh, director of the Center for the Neurobiology of Learning and Memory at the University of California, showed that rats suffered temporary memory loss after stress induction. (McGaugh, 2000)

In his book Brain Longevity, Dharma Singh Khalsa, M.D., describes how older people often have lost 20%

to 25% of the cells in the hippocampus, so that it cannot provide feedback to the hypothalamus. This results in excess production of cortisol (since the feedback loop is not functioning), which in turn damages the hippocampus. He refers to this as a "degenerative cascade." (Singh Khalsa, 1997)

Problems arise when the hippocampus, the area of the brain most damaged by cortisol, is prohibited from engaging in the natural proper feedback loop to the hypothalamus. Normally, the hippocampus signals to the hypothalamus to turn off the cortisol-producing mechanism.

With this feedback loop damaged, cortisol continues to be secreted, creating further damage to the hippocampus and aggravating this cascade. A damaged hippocampus causes cortisol levels to get out of control and incites a degenerative process, which is commonly seen when patients have not found ways to alleviate their stress.

Chronic stress effects the health of cellular regeneration as it interferes with telemere length. Telemeres become shorter with each cellular replication and eventually the cell can't replicate and dies. This accelerates the aging process. (Aubert, 2008)

Stress Memory

As discussed earlier, the "stress memory" also needs to be addressed, not just the original cause of the stress. Although removing the cause by getting out of an abusive relationship for example will alleviate the trigger to the stress feedback loop cycle, the susceptibility remains until the body releases the trauma. This is why some people are so reactive to new situations that "objectively" are not nearly as stressful to the average person.

Deregulation of the HPA axis is implicated in numerous stress-related diseases. HPA axis activity and cytokines are intrinsically intertwined: inflammatory cytokines stimulate the pituitary gland to secrete adrenocorticotropic hormone (ACTH) and cortisol, while glucocorticoids in turn suppress the synthesis of pro-inflammatory cytokines.

Cytokines are known to mediate and control immune and inflammatory responses. Complex interactions exist between cytokines, inflammation and the adaptive responses in maintaining homeostasis.

Chronic secretion of stress hormones, gluco-corticoids, and catecholamines as a result of "disease" may reduce the effect of neurotransmitters, including serotonin, norepinephrine and dopamine, on other receptors in the brain, thereby leading to the deregulation of neurohormones. Glucocorticoids also inhibit the further secretion of corticotropin-releasing hormone from the hypothalamus and ACTH from the pituitary (negative feedback loop.)

The failure of the adaptive systems to resolve inflammation causes a "systemic anti-inflammatory feedback" or "hyperactivity" of the local pro-inflammatory factors, which increases the individual's susceptibility to further degeneration. In fact, laboratory studies have demonstrated that organs and tissues become more vulnerable to inflammation during and after a period of perceived threat, or other stressor. (Chapman et al., 1959)

As discussed earlier, recent research is finding that systemic or neuro-inflammation and neuroimmune activation also play a role in the etiology of a variety of neurodegenerative disorders, such as Parkinson's, Alzheimer's disease, multiple sclerosis, and AIDS-associated dementia.

Given that the brain utilizes 30% of what we consume, what we feed ourselves as well as how we manage our bodies is paramount in addressing stress before our body produces disease states. However, as the development of these disease states is part of a continuum, reversal is always an option. A very first step is to address the body memory of the stress, nourishing the body with foods that will promote repair as well as the use of breathing and relaxation techniques that help to promote homeostasis.

To review, in response to injury, local inflammatory cells (neutrophils, granulocytes and macrophages) secrete a number of cytokines into the bloodstream, most notably the interleukins IL-1, IL-6, and IL-8 and TNF-a.

Likewise, in response to a stress such as shock, the body goes on "alert," setting the sympathetic system into action and triggering the adrenal glands to discharge adrenalin and cortisol. When the perceived threat ends, the body engages the parasympathetic system, which triggers a different set of neurotransmitters and hormones in an attempt to balance the rampages of increased cortisol levels in the brain.

A perceived threat, real or imagined, triggers the

limbic system to respond, via the autonomic nervous system, to regulate metabolism. Even "stress" that is not consciously perceived triggers activity in the attention center of the cerebral cortex, preparing the body for the sympathetic response to stress; that is to say the fight, flight or freeze response, as shown in MRI brain scans. (Franklin Institute, 2011)

Muscles Standing "On Guard"

In light of such a sensitive neuro-immune system, it is not surprising that I see patients come in "wired" with generalized muscle tension which persists long after the initial injury. It appears that there are many mechanisms in play, which fool the body into "believing" that danger is imminent, and that the muscles should stand on guard.

Now looking at the biology behind this process, we know that emotional and cognitive states strongly affect the hypothalamus, a key structure in the nervous system. Surrounded by and interconnected with the limbic system, the part of the nervous system that controls the emotional state of an individual, the hypothalamus, is also adjacent to the cerebral cortex, which provides cognitive and interpretive processes. (Bloom & Lazerson, 2000)

Incoming stimuli are first recognized by the central nervous system (CNS) as a stressor. With repeated exposure, the brain becomes sensitized to these stressors and is more vigilant to incoming stimuli. Stimulated by signals originating inside the body (organs) or outside (i.e. smell, hearing, sight, taste) and by peripheral nerves such as touch, the brain processes stimuli produced by stressful thoughts and emotions, specifically by the hypothalamus. These thoughts and emotions from the cerebral cortex and limbic structures lead to numerous other processes within the brain, as well as in the rest of the body. The entire body is now on the alert for stressors.

Reaction to Stress Stored in Memory

Reactions to all stressors are stored in memory. As stressors are activated or reactivated, the previously conditioned responses are retrieved from memory, primarily by the hippocampus, which is responsible for storing long-term memory. The hippocampus stores memories that are associated with trauma or stress. When a stressful thought reoccurs, the sympathetic nervous system secretes norepinephrine. This neurotransmitter strengthens the stressful memory and activates the stress response.

In essence, each time there is a stressor similar to a previously stored one, the subsequent stressor reinforces the traumatic result from the first stressor. (Bloom & Lazerson, 2000) This is what is meant by your brain is "conditioned" to react to certain stimulus even if the subsequent stimulus is significantly weaker. Sharing this information with patients and making them understand that this process is "scripted in their body" allows them to become "authors" of their own destiny. Mind-body modalities such as meditation, guided imagery or BowenFirst™ can help affect thoughts and emotions through nervous system integration, thus leading to physiological changes.

Early Childhood Trauma & Chronic Disease

The high correlation between early childhood trauma and chronic diseases prompted research on the body's reaction to prolonged versus occasional stress and whether it could be measured through biological indices. "Research shows that the immune system sends signals to the brain that potently alter neural activity and thereby alter everything that flows from neural activity, mainly behaviour, thought and mood," explains Maier.

"In a real, true sense, stress makes you physically sick. In addition, many of the changes over time in mood and cognition from day to day are driven by events in the immune system of which we are unaware." (Azar, 2001)

Untreated chronic stress leads to a systemic inflammatory reaction that disrupts homeostasis. This reaction is mediated by the hypothalamic-pituitary-adrenal axis (HPA axis) and the sympathetic nervous system (SNS).

How Does Stress Become Illness?

As we have seen, stress evokes a complicated cascade of biochemical and physical responses that affect the immune system. The immune system and the brain "talk" to each other through signaling pathways. Mind-body communication is based on physiological pathways that involve the nervous system, the endocrine system, and the immune system.

As numerous studies show, stressors can have profound emotional and physical health consequences. Stressful events trigger cognitive and affective responses, which in turn induce sympathetic nervous system and endocrine changes that ultimately impair immune function. (Chrousos & Gold, 1992, pp.1244-1252)

The immune function is impaired by stress through emotional and/or behavioural manifestations, including anxiety, fear, tension, anger and sadness, as well as in physiological changes, such as heart rate, blood pressure, and sweating. Researchers have suggested that these changes are beneficial if they are of limited duration (Chrousos and Gold, 1992), but when stress is chronic the system is unable to maintain equilibrium, or homeostasis.

Two meta-analyses of the literature show a consistent reduction of immune function in healthy people under stress. The first meta-analysis by Herbert and Cohen in 1993, examined 38 studies of stressful events and immune function in healthy adults. They included studies of acute laboratory stressors (e.g. a speech task), short-term naturalistic stressors (e.g. medical examinations), and long-term naturalistic stressors (e.g. divorce, bereavement, caregiving, and unemployment.)

They found consistent stress-related increases in the numbers of white blood cells, as well as decreases in the numbers of helper T cells, suppressor T cells, and cytotoxic T cells, B cells, and natural killer (NK) cells. This means that there is evident weakening of the immune system, increased susceptibility to chronic inflammatory states and propensity to chronic disease.

The second meta-analysis by Zorrilla et al. in 2001 replicated Herbert and Cohen's work. Using the same study selection procedures, they analyzed 75 studies of stressors and human immunity and came to the same conclusion.

It has been well established that the immune system is susceptible to the cascade of effects produced by stress, but what makes one person's immune system more susceptible? Can stress have statistically measurable and quantifiable consequences to an individual's immune system?

Blauer-Wu recognized that stress is not the only factor that determines how well or poorly the immune system will function. He states, "An individual's ability to cope with stress may be more important than the existence of the stress itself in terms of its effect on health."(Blauer-Wu, 2002, pp167-170)

Different Levels of Coping Skills to Stress

Individuals with high stress levels and excellent coping skills may have minimal effects from stress on the functioning of their immune systems. In contrast, low levels of stress experienced by individuals who have poor coping skills may cause significant alterations in immune functioning, increasing their susceptibility to disease. The actual degree of stress is not as important in determining its effect on the immune system as an individual's coping skills.

Thus, we must ask whether drugs can ever be subtle enough to account for such individual variations? Have we not come full circle with the understanding that the "coping" skills of the individual are paramount? If coping is the best way to alleviate the feedback loop of stress, then all our therapeutic efforts should be placed on understanding this mechanism. Have we ever looked at what increases coping skills? Have we ever considered how proper diet, nutrition and exercise increase the ability to cope with stress? "Coping" is not just a mental activity. It is a biological one.

Personality and behavioural characteristics may also influence an individual's immune response to stress. Passive individuals may have lower cortisol levels, and consequently have fewer alterations in their immune systems in response to stressors.

Perhaps the key to "managing" the immune system depends on personality characteristics and the ability to perceive stress differently. The perception of stress may be the key to triggering the "stress response" in the different hormonal, nervous and immune pathways.

Sickness Behaviour

Once the pathways are triggered, adaptive changes take place resembling "sickness behaviour." The term "sickness behaviour" has been identified in the reactions of individuals during the course of an infection. Lethargy, depression, loss of appetite, anxiety, social withdrawal, and failure to concentrate characterize the behaviour.

Acute psychosocial stress can trigger the same pathways and cause the same symptoms as infection does, again leading to the "sickness behaviour." As we have seen, this process is mediated through cytokines that affect the brain directly. Brydon et.al., conclude in their study that, "Acute psychosocial stress enhances the ability of an immune response to trigger both inflammation and behavioural sickness."(Brydon, 2009) Andrews suggests that as the body uses fever to fight infection, the brain may also be using depression to fight unusual stress. (Andrews, 2011)

It seems to me that without this knowledge we may be misinterpreting the body's own self-regulatory abilities. Thus the conventional prescription of anti-inflammatories or anti-depressants would be contra-indicated, as they would impede this process.

Furthermore, Andrews writes, "There's a lot of debate about whether or not depression is truly a disorder, as most clinicians and the majority of the psychiatric establishment believe, or whether it's an evolved adaptation that does something useful."

Longitudinal studies demonstrate that more than 40% of the population may experience major depression at some point in their lives, triggered by traumatic events, such as the death of a loved one, the end of a relationship or the loss of a job. Andrews says the brain may defer other functions, such as appetite, sex drive, sleep and social connectivity, in order to focus on coping with the traumatic event.

I have found in my practice that therapies that enhance the ability of the body to achieve this homeostasis are far more useful and effective than those that suppress this natural coping mechanism.

It is also plausible, as Dr. Daniel Amen has found, that many states of anxiety and depression are a result of nutritional deficiencies, sometimes as common as insufficient vitamin D. Verified through the use of functional brain scans, Amen has been able to illustrate brain transformation after use of proper nutrition. (See his website: www.amenclinics.com/meet-dr-amen)

Undoubtedly, the "mind-body" connection exists, not merely in theory but in clearly identified biological pathways. Accordingly, thorough assessment of a client's condition must involve an understanding of their emotional and physical states. In particular, taking into account potential stressors in a patient's life as well as their coping mechanisms will usually provide invaluable information for assessment.

My Story with MS :

I want to share with you the life-changing consequences of my encounters with Multiple Sclerosis ("MS"). But first, a disclaimer: I hope that I have made it very clear in this telling that just as there is no such thing as the "right" life journey for everyone, neither is there a single, prescribed path for recovery.

Furthermore, it is my personal and professional observation that healing is a kind of movement through ascending levels of consciousness -- each upward step increasing our perceptions of what is possible, not only physically but also spiritually, and naturally incorporating what is needed by that particular individual at that particular time.

Where there is flow and movement, there is opportunity for change.

There are many forces at play in the healing process, but two emotions are constantly surfacing—fear and love. Confronted with change, fear is reflexively defensive, but love is open and accepting.

Fear of the possibility of loss makes us hold more tightly onto what we possess. A rigid hostility to any change underlies a fragile sense of security. "Better the devil you know than the one you don't."

Love on the other hand, is light and expansive. It's an expression of our trust in the ultimate goodness of the world, and of our sense of all things having their place in the universe. Love makes life feel like a continuum, and a soul's journey in the body feel as part of a greater whole.

Consciousness expands when we pay close attention and accept whatever happens to our perceptions as we accumulate life experience and expose ourselves to knowledge. We must be careful though, for knowledge is worthless without the interpreter.

For example, I have often recommended Gabor Mate's book, "When the Body Says No" to many of my patients as an excellent source of knowledge. But I find that without the right support, you won't have the strength to face the important issues and will fail to feel empowered to change your patterns.

Most of my MS patients shared these characteristics: weak personal boundaries, dysfunctional relation-ships, history of physical or emotional abuse, prefer putting the needs of others before self, an inordinate need for affection and love, feelings of inadequacy due to perceived inability to cope, and in the midst of grieving or other emotional upset.

When I first got MS, I was 21. A sudden bout of optic neuritis sent me to an ophthalmologist, as I thought I had cut my eye with my contact lenses. My eye was blinded and the pain did not allow me to easily open it; when I did, I saw double.

The ophthalmologist reassured me that my eye was not cut; I went back to my apartment and waited until the pain would go away. The entire incident lasted four days.

It never occurred to me that the symptoms were an indication of anything more serious, and "braving" the pain felt like a reasonable solution in the circumstances. Nothing more came of this, other than the ophthalmologist's subsequent observation that I had a slight tremor typical of neurological damage, often seen in MS or Parkinson.

Twelve years later the realization of a deep lack of expressed love and affection in my life finally hit me with tremendous force. I had married a man who still loved me, but who was unable to express it in a way that satisfied my yearnings.

Please remember that what follows is simply my perception of the relationship. There will be no faultfinding or blame, only the facts as honestly and accurately as I can perceive and express them.

Now, whether or not he expressed his love for me, I was unable to perceive it, nor receive it. All I know is that I was withering away. I wrote poems of a rose dying before it had blossomed, and of a rose dying from neglect. I was totally passive in the expectation that love would come from him, and that I was helpless to change anything at all.

I began to wonder whether I had asked too much of life, whether I should just accept the situation and learn to live without love. Of course, in the beginning I was happily convinced that my marriage met all that was required in a proper match, but now nothing alleviated the feeling that I was not sufficiently loved.

I had not yet realized that this feeling was an "old" emotion that had its origins in my childhood. I sincerely believed back then that I wasn't loved because I wasn't understood. As usually happens in an adolescent girl's life, this attitude was triggered by my relationship with my mother. She regarded me as a challenge merely to keep up with, let alone understand or control. Of course, I was just going through the usual travails of a young teenager, ignorant of what being a mother to someone like me was like for someone like her.

She did love me of course, but I felt none of it. The net result is that I felt hopelessly misunderstood. I refused to see the love I was given as genuine, and was blind to the emotional and developmental consequences of equating love with being understood. One consequence was a "real" sense of not being loved for whom I was and not getting the affection I felt I deserved from my husband.

And so, in the summer of 1995, I experienced tingling and numbness in my legs, a symptom that was greatly aggravated by warm baths. I kept losing my balance due to the weakness I felt in my legs. It was as if they had even lost the strength to keep me standing.

The history, the symptoms and the neurological exam results (ie. Hyper-excitable reflexes, inability to walk foot to heel in a straight-line, hyper-sensitivity to heat) all led to my diagnosis. I decided to pass up an MRI since at most it could only confirm the presence of demyelination, which would merely confirm the diagnosis.

Just as an aside, demyelination occurs in other conditions than just MS. Furthermore, demylenation alone does not necessarily produce symptoms.

By that point I had already seen several patients with MS and I was aware that the treatment choices were very limited and mostly experimental, and that most of the patients who had joined "support groups" fared much worse than those who knew less of their condition. Because I could not pretend I was unaware of the prognosis for my condition, all I could do was to defy it, instead of letting it define me.

So, what was this "condition"? I drew up a picture of myself, including the symptoms that I was experiencing on both the physiological and emotional levels. About six weeks prior to the onset of the physical symptoms, I started to prefer spending time alone and was not keen on friends visiting, which was totally inconsistent with my more bubbly personality. I readily overheated in the sun and wanted to stay out of it. I had an increased thirst for cold water and craved meat, salt and pasta.

I felt generally worse around 6 p.m. after I started to develop those physical symptoms. The treatment I chose was homeopathy as I had experience with it and believed that my symptoms fell easily into a recognizable treatment protocol. The remedy I took encompassed all the symptoms mentioned, as well as ailments resulting from disappointed love.

I took the homeopathic prescription and repeated each time any of the above symptoms returned until there was no further need for treatment.

The prognosis looked good as I responded in a predictable way, highlighting to me all my emotional states. It was like watching a movie of my life, but with a bit of distance. There was a gap created in which consciousness crept in, and with it, healing. My journey and the synthesized journeys I shared through my one to one process with patients has now finally been structured into my LISTEN to your body" program. There are key patterns and simple steps that we share in common when we experience chronic disease. I will elaborate more about this in the final chapter.

Taking the remedy freed me of the symptoms so that I was able to consciously throw myself back into the marriage and give it another chance. The relationship did not last in the end, but I came out of it whole.

For numerous reasons, many that were circumstantial, and many because the timing was wrong, it was clear that we were not a match. What I gained from the experience was the ability to drop the feeling that I had somehow failed. I also was freed from the self-justifications I was clinging to in my story of unrequited love, and was able to stop blaming myself, and him, for the situation we found ourselves living in.

The result of this insight allowed me to emotionally separate from my husband and to realize that he was likely going through a process that was truly his own and which had nothing to do with me. I could now accept that he required space to experience that.

Not having clear boundaries at the time, I believed that his experience was directly related to mine. That is why I had taken things so personally before the onset of the disease. For example, if he was withdrawn,

I would take it as a form of rejection. If he was sad, I'd be sad, even though I didn't know why. And if he was happy, I was certain I had done something to make it so. Basically, I was passively enmeshed in my perception of his reality; my nervous system was stuck in a reactive mode, and I no longer could trust myself to "stand" independently.

Over the past 17 years, I have had three recurrences of these symptoms, each one corresponding to a period of perceived stress. Each time it was gone in less than a week, and twice in just two days; all I had to do was remind my being and system of the "state" I was revisiting.

The predisposition to view the world as I originally did still lives in me, but today it clearly is a "recognizable state." I no longer confuse it as a reflection of all of me. It no longer defines me, in the same way that the symptoms of MS serve as a reminder of that fragility, but do not define how my body needs to act.

When I look at my results and those of patients who have done well in managing their MS, and I compare them to those who have had a harder time with it, I see one important distinction. Those who did not do well kept getting retriggered by an unsupportive environment, which made the transformation more difficult. They also "chose" to listen to fear and did not embrace the vast open field of possibilities that come with embracing love.

The ones who did well were able to free themselves from the repeated experience of the perceived stress during their healing. They either eliminated the perceived stress, or else learned to perceive the stress differently so that it gave up its hold on them.

As Byron Katie has stated so eloquently, "…it only takes one to be happy in a relationship."

Circumstances changed for some of these patients; for others, it was just a change in their ways of perceiving which allowed them to move forward in their lives. This was accomplished by increasing their awareness and by reminding their bodies of the healing path.

These experiences left me with a greater sense of autonomy and independence from the emotional "expression" of others. Instead of retreating and putting up walls to "protect myself" from the emotional pain of unrequited love, I was free to experience the dynamic without the self-sabotage program running in the background.

My journey and the synthesized journeys I shared through my one-to-one process with patients has now finally been structured into my "LISTEN to your body" program. There are key patterns and simple steps that we share in common when we experience chronic disease. I will elaborate more about this in the final chapter.

I was free to make choices that were loving to myself and I was free to leave without animosity or ill feeling when the relationship finally ended.

I made those choices, and so I became what I needed to become. The healing that transpired not only healed my MS, my story of the past but grew me into the person that knew profoundly that what one feels they lack is what one is not able to give to oneself. It was a huge discovery which changed my interactions and made me more inwardly-reflective rather than looking at others as a source to fill my void.

Assessment Part Three

The Faces of the Pain Chameleon

Pain is a good example of the conundrum doctors' face with regard to "assessment." The experience of pain is subjective, and the objective qualifiers, such as X-rays and MRIs, do not give us much insight. "Findings" of pain at the tissue level often do not correlate with the pain experience.

Given how little is really known about pain, the real problem is the lack of research in solutions for pain management or treatment. In fact, the usefulness of the term "chronic pain" has recently been questioned, since the duration of pain is less relevant than multifactorial components, which are subjective at best. The risk factors and low response rate of surgeries, as well as the statistically insignificant advantages from pain medication, demonstrate that helping people who are experiencing pain is in its infancy. As Assessment is required prior to the Plan, what can we offer these patients?

In light of the recent research on techniques and modalities or approaches that deal with pain, I can comfortably say that I would be terribly discouraged if it were not for my clinical experience.

The philosophy of my clinic, the "prime directive" so to speak, is to deal with the pain first. Despite the beneficial health sustaining and health-promoting methods available, I have found in my practice that people suffering from pain are focused primarily on obtaining relief for their pain.

Perhaps the most effective way of addressing the multifactorial, psycho-physical condition, which manifests in various parts of the body and with varying degrees of intensity, is with BowenFirst™ treatments. This treatment is like a body language translator that allows the therapist to follow the signals the body is giving. This therapy involves using gentle touch to allow the body to let go of its "stuck" patterns of pain and restriction.

It is as though, in a self-protective effort, which at first may have been warranted, the body got "stuck" protecting the body part with pain, calcification, inflammation or swelling -all attempts to immobilize the damaged joint. The pattern outlives the actual damage, and thus with a simple touch, the body is "rebooted," first by un-programming the pain pathways, and then by reminding the body that it can heal.

Maybe there is something else that is being transmitted through the "simple touch" of hands that the body laps up so ravenously? James Oschman points out that the wall of connective tissue around an injury (the defenses) does not need to be there if there are enough electrons in the ground substance to neutralize the free radicals. He believes that the walling off, is a defense of the body when it is electron-nutrient deficient (Oschman, 2003)

Treating Pain with BowenFirst ™

I have successfully treated patients using BowenFirst™ for frozen shoulders, sciatica, migraines, low back pain, whiplash, TMJ and fibromyalgia, as well as for generalized aches and pains with their various reasons and likely "explanation" as in osteoarthritis years after a sports injury, or pain of unknown origin and of variable intensity.

I have seen a patient who was suffering from a "frozen shoulder" for five to seven years in a couple of treatments regain complete mobility, as well as swollen joints that promptly give up protective swelling and move freely, and a neck held rigid by calcification find mobility and allow the body to reabsorb the osteophytes. I have also seen BowenFirst™ successfully treat emotional pain which can take the form of anxiety, depression, ADHD and OCD.

In just 3 to 5 sessions, most patients experience relief. The treatment is gentle, does not require effort on their part, and yields results of 50% to 80% improvement by the third session and 100% by the fifth session in 85% of patients.

In patients who have been on strong opioids, like morphine, results are varied, possibly because they have reduced sensitivity to experience the input from the treatment. Patients taking muscle relaxants or using methods that artificially and temporarily achieve a short-term functional goal (i.e. relaxing the muscle without teaching the muscle how to relax on its own), may require additional treatments to see results; however, most patients have a very quick turn-around period.

As BowenFirst™ is a fairly new approach, the mechanisms of its actions are not all understood. Research would be very welcome as it would allow patients to understand the mechanisms involved and seek some comfort in what at this point appears to many as a "miracle."

Let's look at today's pain research and maybe shed some light on the status quo.

What is Pain Anyway?

The International Association for the Study of Pain (IASP) defines pain as, "An unpleasant sensory and emotional experience associated with actual or potential tissue damage, or described in terms of such." Note that by definition, pain is always subjective. Each of us learns the application of the term through experiences related to injury in early life. Pain is that experience we associate with actual or potential tissue damage. "It is unquestionably a sensation in part or parts of the body, and it is always unpleasant—and therefore it is also an emotional experience." (IASP)

Unpleasant, abnormal experiences, "dysesthesia," are not necessarily painful by IASP's definition because they may not have the usual sensory qualities of pain. This means that pain perception is conditioned. In certain circumstances stimuli not normally perceived as painful can be recorded as extremely painful. Alterations in the central nervous system (neural sensitization) have also been suggested as an explanation for the persistence of pain. (Purves, 2004, pp.209- 228)

How Does My Brain Register Pain?

The pathways for pain transmission are complex.

Generally, nociceptive (pain-info) information reports external and internal representation of the body's physiological condition through two different components:

1. The sensory-discriminative component, transmitted through the spinothalamic tract, is relayed via the thalamus to reach the somato-sensory cortex and associated areas.
2. The spinobrachial pathways have connections to brain regions involved in the affective-emotioal component. The affective and motivational reactions to noxious stimuli are then mediated to several different centers in the brain.

Basically, there is a "touch and feel" passage, and a "remember the feeling" pathway.

It is well known that the subjective response to a given pain stimulus varies because of neuronal modulation. The "gate control" theory (Wall and Melzack, 1989) has formed a basis for the description of this mechanism. Thus, the ascending noci-ceptive information may be modulated by both peripheral inputs and several central mechanisms. "Neuronal plasticity" means that the neurons involved in pain transmission are converted from a state of normosensitivity to one in which they are hypersensitive. This is why a person who received a serious burn often is far more sensitized to the effects of sun after that initial experience.

We now know that pathways involving higher centers,

such as the dorsolateral prefrontal cortex, may evoke both facilitating and inhibitory influence on nociceptive transmission, and thus on the pain perception (Pertovaara, 2000; Lorenz et al., 2003).This modulation is effectuated by neurochemical mediators. Important examples are the endogenous opioid and NMDA (N-methyl-D-aspartate) receptors.

Purves et al, explain how the increased activity of the NMDA receptor can amplify the pain impulse coming from the periphery. This is known as the "wind-up phenomenon." (Sandkulher, 2000) The consequence can be central sensitization and hyper-excitability, which may increase the sensitivity to pain impulses in the whole spinal cord. "The result of such modulation can be hyperalgesia (an extreme or heightened reaction to a stimulus that normally provokes pain) and allodynia, which means pain from a stimulus that normally does not lead to the sensation of pain and often occurs after injury to that site." (Purves et. al, 2004,p.209-228)

Perceived Pain and Degree of Sensitivity

What this amounts to is that we cannot link the two phenomena (ie. the lesion/trauma and the degree of perceived pain) in a reliable way. The effect of this discovery is that policy-making criteria for disability needs to become less dismissive of people's perceived pain. Although we may be able to understand some of the neuronal modulations and pathways, we can only surmise the degree of sensitivity felt, and there is a big gap when it comes to "lesion-proof." Therapeutically, emphasis on pain-killers may actually miss the mark as there is more to the story.

To take neck pain as an example, Ferrari found that it can seldom be attributed to any specific origin and is often labeled as soft-tissue rheumatism or muscular/mechanical/postural neck pain, or other unspecific syndromes (Ferrari, 2003,pp. 57-70). Furthermore, Boden and later on Matsumoto established in their respective studies that clinical and radiographic examinations seldom showed organic lesions to be responsible for the symptoms in neck pain (Boden et al., 1990; Matsumoto et al., 1998). Instead, psychosocial and cultural factors have been proposed to be contributory factors.

More recently, psychological factors have also been associated with poor prognosis. A number of authors have demonstrated the important role of psychological and psychosocial factors in determining the outcome of whiplash injury including perceived pain interference, general psychological distress and emotional problems. Further, Hendriks et al (2005,pp. 114408-16) report that an increasing somatization score is associated with lack of functional recovery at 12 months and is more important etiologically than are collision-specific factors (Atherton, K, et al; 2006.pp.196-206)

Solid Matter is not Fixed

I will never forget the patient I saw in Stouffville, Ontario who was told by her chiropractor that the pain and lack of motion in her neck had to do with the osteophytes that had amassed on her cervical spine. After two series of 30 ineffective treatments, she came to see me and asked if there was anything I could do to help her. First of all, I explained to her that the osteophytes had likely appeared in an attempt to mobilize the neck in response to the original injury. I told her that when we address the original injury by allowing the body to rewire, the body would quickly re-absorb the osteophytes.

I gave her a treatment and to my surprise, having seen her x-ray, she was able to move her head laterally almost 80 degrees to both sides, a great improvement from the 30 degrees she came in with. I suggested she get another x-ray to see if we could find evidence of the osteophytes disappearing. The x-ray was identical. This was one of the first times that I recognized that "solid" matter is not fixed.

I treated her one more time, and at her sixth month x-ray there was no evidence of osteophytes. It took between two weeks and six months for the body to reabsorb them. But she was pain free and with full mobility right from the second visit on. How much impact did her understanding that her body was doing the best it could and just on overdrive, free her to allow for mobility? It was clear that when she felt that the osteophytes were a limiting factor, she had little room for improvement.

Tension and physical stress may also prolong the chronic pain state (Turk, 1996), but this does not necessarily cause the pain directly — rather, it is the distress, which exacerbates or complicates the pain, thereby hindering its natural resolution (Turk, 1996). Turk explains this in the following excerpt from his research:

"When we review studies of predictors of recovery versus continued disability, we find that maladaptive attitudes and beliefs, lack of social support, heightened emotional reactivity, job dissatisfaction, substance abuse, compensation status, and the prevalence of pain behaviours (e.g., Turk, 1997) and psychiatric diagnosis (Gatchel & Epker, 1999) appear to be among the best predictors of the transition from acute injury to chronic disability. It is interesting to note that physical factors, including severity of injury and physical demands of the job, do not appear to contribute as much to the prediction of chronicity." (Turk, 2002, p. 681)

Whiplash and Muscle Damage

There is even a body of research that has found that chronic neck pain after whiplash injuries does not appear to result from muscle damage (Barnsley,1994, pp. 283-307; Whiplash Commission, 2005) There is no strong evidence that whiplash trauma leads to injury of the nervous system, and studies have found that only a small proportion of individuals enduring high-impact whiplash trauma are affected in this way. (Guez et al., 2003, pp. 576-9; Hildingsson et al., 1993)

In other words, the cognitive complaints have not been clearly linked to any predictable structural correlates of morphological or functional brain damage or even to measurable impaired cognitive performance. Instead, Radanov and others claim that the injury itself may trigger emotional and cognitive symptoms (Radanov, 1999), which has been linked to personality. (Vendrig, 2000)

Somatization, in combination with inadequate ability to cope, may play a role in the development, persistence, or aggravation of whiplash-related symptoms, such as pain or cognitive dysfunction. (Bosma et al., 2002, pp 56-65)

Few insightful studies demonstrate successful treatments for chronic neck pain. Apart from whiplash injuries, other types of trauma may also result in chronic neck pain. Furthermore, it is not known whether a traumatic origin for chronic neck pain—especially whiplash injury—has any influence on the character of pain itself.

So once again, all I can share is that in my experience that it is important to maintain normal tissue mobility. It is helpful psychologically to reinforce commitment to the healing process and also improve functionality. Tissue mobility is critical in addressing pain, especially to avoid it becoming chronic. Enhanced mobility can help normalize vascular flow, decrease the buildup of metabolic waste, increase lymphatic flow and decrease swelling, freeing normal neural structure and function.

It can also decrease adaptive body patterns that might be maintaining chronic pain signals, and normalize autonomic nervous system function, thus decreasing abnormal strain on the associated somatic and visceral structures. To achieve tissue mobility, it is essential to break these maladaptive patterns and have the person recognize these changes so as to start reinforcing positive feedback loops.

Pain and ANS Deregulation

As we have covered previously, the autonomic nervous system (ANS) is comprised of both the parasympathetic and sympathetic nervous system. We have seen that in chronic stress, the sympathetic system, through several hormonal and neural pathways, maintains a state of chronic stress.

While sympathetic activation is a normal and adaptive response to stress, chronic sympathetic activation, characterized by heightened physical and psychological responses, can develop in the presence of relentless stressors. (Boscarino, 1996; Lepore, Miles, & Levy, 1997; McEwen, 1998) Nociception, or pain perception, has been demonstrated as one of the most significant activators of the sympathetic nervous system (Guyton & Hall, 2006), and emotional stress can also lead to sympathetic activation. (Lepore et al., 1997; McEwen & Stellar, 1993; Robinson & Riley, 1999)

Research conducted on temporomandibular disorders (TMD) in order to establish whether Autonomic Nervous System (ANS) deregulation is a defining feature of TMD, examined the physiological and psychological differences between chronic TMD patients and pain-free controls. (Schmidt & Carlson, 2009) As both nociception and psychological distress are central to chronic pain conditions, it is not unreasonable to expect that patients with chronic TMD would likely suffer from sustained activation of the ANS.

The research conducted by Schmidt and Carlson found that, "TMD patients showed significantly more physiological activation and emotional reactivity during the baseline and recovery periods than the control participants. This suggests that TMD patients are not unique in the way they react to a particular stressor, but are unique in their experience of ANS deregulation, which presents as prolonged sympathetic activation. This is why during the baseline and recovery periods their physiological markers were elevated as compared to the control group." (Schmidt and Carlson 2009 pp. 230-242)

So in other words, regardless of whether ANS deregulation is activated by physical or psychological triggers, such activation may have significant effects on nociceptive transmission and subsequent pain experiences.

So which comes first, the chicken or the egg? Are some people more primed for pain because of deregulation of the ANS or does the pain experience prime their ANS for dysfunction? The authors conclude, "Thus, although it is unclear whether physiological deregulation is a consequence and/or causative factor in an individual's chronic pain experience, better self-regulation of physiological activation can be regarded as an important treatment goal for persons with TMD and other chronic pains." And in such lies the beauty of therapeutics that are aimed at regulating the ANS.

According to Carver & Scheier, (1982, 1998) "Self-regulation theory is a useful framework to address the physiological deregulation that contributes to the physical and psychological problems reported by TMD patients." The "self-regulatory theory" is an approach to health management that strongly engages the patients' will to implement the advice given. The belief is founded on the understanding that for medical treatments to be effective, the patient needs to be interested in improving their own health.

After reading this research I was better able to understand how pivotal the TMJ protocol and the Vaso-Vagal protocols in BowenFirst™ actually are. Through the body portal, the patient feels the profound release of their stress and sees, for the first time ever, in the majority of cases, a hope for change. It is much easier to be interested in improving ones health when one has a reason to believe that there is hope.

Are We Prescribing Chronic Pain?

Patients seeking care for pain want to know whether their pain is likely to improve or run a chronic course, not just its cause and how it might be relieved and managed. But it is difficult for the doctor to give a clear and reassuring answer. "Physicians' abilities to provide guidance regarding pain's likely course, as well as clinical and epidemiologic research, are hampered by lack of clear-cut, evidence-based operational criteria for classifying chronic pain." (Van Korff & Dunn, 2008, 267-276)

How chronic pain is initiated, maintained and prolonged is the crucial question in the field of pain research. Apparently, there is not always a direct association between tissue damage, pain perception and behaviour. While acute pain has a clear and understandable biological function and keeps one out of harm's way, as seen with the reflex reaction to putting one's hand on the hot stove, chronic pain without any recognizable tissue injury does not appear to serve any purpose for the individual.

The International Association for the Study of Pain defines chronic pain as, ''...pain which persists past the normal time of healing... With non-malignant pain, three months is the most convenient point of division between acute and chronic pain, but for research purposes, six months will often be preferred." (Van Korff & Dunn, 2008)

Defining chronic pain solely by duration is based on the view that acute pain signals potentiate tissue damage, whereas chronic pain results from central and peripheral sensitization, in which pain is sustained after nociceptive inputs have diminished.

Van Korff & Dunn argue that "while conceptually appealing, this approach has not produced reliable or valid methods for differentiating acute from chronic pain for clinical or epidemiological research, nor has it led to practical operational criteria for identifying chronic pain in clinical practice. Defining chronic pain solely by duration does not indicate whether long-lasting pain is clinically significant, and duration-based definitions can be difficult to apply to recurrent pain."(Van Korff & Dunn, 2008)

For these reasons, Korff and Dunn, in "Chronic Pain Reconsidered" re-examine how chronic pain is defined. They argue that, "the term chronic pain is as much a prognostic statement as a description of pain history. "(2008)

Von Korff and Miglioretti recently proposed defining

chronic back pain prospectively, using a Risk Score to predict the likelihood that clinically significant pain is present at a future time point. The Risk Score approach suggests that chronic pain should be defined by the likelihood that clinically significant pain will continue in the future, not only by how long pain has lasted.

As we have seen, the term chronic has been defined traditionally solely by pain duration, yet there are many more factors that contribute to the state of chronicity. Furthermore, the word "chronic" implies an unchanging condition, which "chronic pain" is not. However, as many practicing clinicians recognize, predicting whether pain will run a chronic course is not simply a matter of determining pain's duration. A patient who limits activities and reports depressive symptoms and pain at diffuse anatomical locations may fit a clinician's intuitive chronic pain profile better than a patient with long-lasting pain not accompanied by other unfavorable prognostic indicators.

In their research, Korff et al. observed a continuum of chronic pain, with no distinct class of chronic pain patients. No clear demarcation distinguished persons with possible or probable chronic pain from those with less significant and enduring pain. They state, "Chronic pain should be viewed as a condition whose future implications are inherently uncertain and mutable, rather than as a fixed trait identifying patients with intractable pain.

"The potential for change, indeed the likelihood of change, is an important and oft-neglected feature of chronic pain. For these reasons, the terms possible and probable chronic pain, appropriately emphasize the inherent uncertainty of long-term pain outcomes, with improvement always possible."

This approach shifts the focus from the potentially stigmatizing labeling of "chronic pain patients" to the likelihood of steps that might reduce future risks of significant pain and dysfunction.

The authors conclude by saying, "By broadening the defining features of chronic pain to include factors other than pain duration, both clinicians and patients may become more aware of opportunities to improve outcomes when pain continues past the normal time of healing."

Current Drugs Prescribed for Pain

Animal models for chronic pain have their shortcomings, despite some pioneering work in the late '70s and mid-80s. At minimum and for our purposes, these animal models have at least confirmed that chronic pain states are biological entities and not just the imagination of patients. Moreover, they allow for a mechanistic study of pathophysiology, and this has been a fantastic boon to understanding the peripheral and spinal cord mechanisms underlying various types of chronic pain. Where these models fall short, however, is in many clinical conditions where the actual correspondence between the purported model and the clinical manifestation remains to be directly tested and seen.

"As a result," write Korff et al., "We are often unsure

if these models are providing actual specific mechanistic information or even general hints as to the possible list of mechanisms that may underlie the true clinical condition. In chronic back pain, for example, do models of peripheral nerve injury provide insights into symptoms of back pain? What about skin or muscle inflammation? Another shortcoming is their inability to dispel suspicion regarding more complex conditions, such as CRPS and fibromyalgia, for which we do not even know how to begin building animal models.

Thus in many respects the initial excitement that these models provided regarding the opportunity for designing new therapies for clinical pain conditions has already waned. It is now almost 20 years since the Bennett CCI model, and despite over a hundred peripheral and central molecular targets having been generated from these models and large sums of research dollars invested by pharmaceutical companies, we have yet to identify any new therapy based on an animal model for neuropathic pain." (Van Korff & Dunn, 2008)

A 2000 meta-analysis of NSAID studies found no evidence that these drugs were effective in treating chronic low back pain. (van Tulder et al., 2000) "More recent treatment studies have also failed to reach clinical effectiveness, with most only finding about a 10% decrease in pain." (Coats et al., 2004; Pallay et al., 2004)

Drugs and Chronic Back Pain

A systematic review of antidepressants treatment for chronic back pain also concluded that they produce only a moderate symptom reduction (Staiger et al., 2003), and another recent review concluded that many drugs used for back pain are no more, or only slightly more, effective than placebos. Others have side effects that outweigh their usefulness in relieving pain. On the basis of the evidence, no drug regimen can be legitimately recommended for back pain." (Bogduk, 2004) The World Health Organization Advisory Panel likewise concluded that there is no single treatment superior to others for relieving chronic back pain. (Ehrlich, 2003)

Similarly, researchers Wand and O'Connell have commented on the "epiphenomena: [Chronic back pain] patients have back pain yet no conservative or surgical pain-relieving measures directed at the back appear effective. They display a number of biomechanical abnormalities, however treatment directed at normalizing lumbar biomechanics has little effect, and there is no relationship between changes in outcome and changes in spinal mechanics. Finally, these patients demonstrate some psychological problems, but psychologically-based treatments offer only a partial solution to the problem. A possible explanation for these findings is that they are epiphenomena, features that are incidental to a problem of neurological reorganisation and degeneration." (Wand and O'Connell, 2008)

Looking at the studies, it is possible that the frame of reference may be too small to see the bigger picture — that people who have experienced pain can be pain -free and that a comprehensive approach combining manual therapy, fascial work, nutritional support and humanistic doctor-patient relationships may just be the key.

Pain: A Mind-Body Connection

As psychoneuroimmunology offers a conceptual and biological understanding of the mind-body connections, pain and the concept of pain have evolved from a purely biomedical approach to a multi-dimensional understanding. Several authors have categorized management and treatment approaches, which backed by research, have given us a broader definition and understanding of pain.

Two approaches, "biopsychosocial" and the "phenomenological perspective," (as well as the consideration that despite the increased perception and understanding of chronic pain phenomena, treatment solutions have yet to be explained by these or other process), will be discussed below.

Engel (1977) introduced the term biopsychosocial as a broad construct to convey the importance of considering the interacting roles that biological/physical, psychological, and social factors play in illness and disease. J. Loeser, in his book Concepts of Pain (1982), draws distinctions between the four dimensions of pain experience: nociception, pain perception, suffering, and pain behaviour. (Loeser, 1982) First, nociception, which refers to stimulation of the nerves that convey information about tissue damage to the brain, accounts for the 'bio' part of 'biopsychosocial.' In the treatment of TMD, a biomedical reductionist approach limits its focus to addressing nociceptive inputs, using traditional dental and medical treatments, such as splints and analgesic medications. However, a 1:1 correlation between tissue damage and patients' pain experience is rarely observed. To illustrate, reports of pain in the absence of tissue damage is common among psychiatric patients (Chaturvedi, 1987), and pain can persist after the healing of tissue in conditions such as causalgia and phantom limb syndrome. (Melzack, 1973)

Thus, a second dimension to consider is pain perception, which is a complex subjective experience that involves sensory input being filtered through an individual's genetic composition, prior learning, psychological status, and sociocultural influences. The distinction between nociception and pain perception can be likened to the distinction between disease (objective biological event involving the disruption of specific body structures) and illness (subjective experience of disease.)

The third dimension characterizing an individual's pain experience is suffering, which refers to the emotional (e.g. anxiety, anger) and cognitive (e.g. thoughts of helplessness) responses to pain perception. It is important to assess an individual's emotional reactions to and cognitions about pain, because they can influence recovery."(Loeser, 1982, pp. 109-142) Suffering is an affective response generated in higher nervous centers by pain, or by other affective states such as depression, isolation, fear or anxiety. The limbic lobes of the brain are critically involved in suffering. This means that suffering is contextual by nature.

Pain Behaviour

The fourth dimension Loeser talks about is "pain behaviour." Pain behaviours are the things a person says or does, or does not do, that suggest that tissue damage has occurred. Pain behaviours are closely linked to the expression of suffering. For example, it can be seen in expressions like moaning, limping, and avoidance of certain activities. "Pain behaviours are a subset of illness behaviours and they always reflect more than tissue damage." (Loeser, 1982)

Cognition and fear avoidance beliefs such as catastrophizing and passive coping are strongly related to pain and disability, and reduce the capacity to handle chronic pain. (Linton, 2000)

For example, increased disability is associated with beliefs that pain is a sign of damage, that activity should be avoided when one has pain, and that pain is permanent. (Balderson, Lin & Von Korff, 2004). "Similarly, pain patients who are depressed may have little motivation to comply with treatment recommendations (Von Korff & Simon, 1996), and those with anxiety may be afraid to engage in day-to-day activities out of fear that doing so will exacerbate their pain."(Vlaeyen, Kole-Snijders, Rotteveel, Ruesink, & Heuts, 1995) In sum, people's affective and cognitive responses to pain have the potential to negatively influence the course of their pain condition.

An individual's beliefs about pain, emotional experience, and pain behaviour are interrelated. For instance, behavioiral experience can show patients they are capable of participating in their regular, daily activities, and reduce thoughts of helplessness and negative emotions. (Vlaeyen et al., 2002) Additionally, some cognitive coping strategies (e.g., problem solving, goal setting) can increase an individual's self-efficacy regarding the control of emotional and behavioural responses. (Samwel, Evers, Crul, & Kraaimaat, 2006; Turner & Romano, 2001) Taking into account the four dimensions of pain experience (nociception, pain perception, suffering, and pain behaviour), the biopsychosocial approach to managing chronic pain is an improvement to the biomedical approach.

In a one-year follow-up study on the effects of a personal construct group-learning program on patients with chronic musculoskeletal pain, researchers Eldri Steen and Liv Haugli (2001) found that lack of control and inefficient coping with internal and external demands contribute to pain and pain behaviour.

While Steen and Haugli state that treatment programs do exist that approach chronic pain from a psychological point of view, promoting educational pain programs, as well as cognitive understanding of pain and pain models, in order for behaviours to be modified, has been met with limited success. Steen and Haugli (2001) approach their own pilot project and one-year follow-up with a "phenomenological perspective" where the individual experience of their situation is essential. The basic precept is that the body is not regarded as a material object, but rather as "our centre and carrier of meaning, and we live and experience meaning directly in our bodies." (Haugli, 2000)

Thus, when assessing pain, we must look at each

patient as an individual, taking into account their physical, emotional and mental states. We need to look at all presenting symptoms, including the story behind the parable as well as the chameleon-like nature of pain and stressors.

We must be guided toward the Plan by a deep understanding and reflection with the patient on the meaning of the symptoms experienced by them. It is the patient who will know in their heart whether they require knowing the "cause," and the underpinnings of the "cure" and whether they can stay perplexed, open and curious.

Chapter Four

Plan: Beyond Glorified Coping Skills and the Placebo Effect

"Medicine tells us as much about the meaningful performance of healing, suffering and dying as chemical analysis tells us about the aesthetic value of pottery."

Ivan Ilyich in Limits to Medicine

"We confine ourselves to a narrow realm indeed if we exclude from accepted knowledge the contributions of human experience and insight."

Gabor Mate

Assessment involves more than making a diagnosis. A complete assessment includes a determination about what will be of greatest value to the patient when it comes to prescribing treatment.

Each doctor's prescription will depend on their underlying philosophy about healing: Do the expression of the patient's symptoms require a disease category, or are they signs that the body is out of balance and requires some recalibration? This will determine whether you categorize the symptomatology into "disease entities" or "symptom management," requiring prescriptions, either on the biological level (as in antibiotics, anti-inflammatories), or emotional level (such as antipsychotics), or whether you fundamentally believe that the body responds to its multifaceted environment and needs help to achieve homeostasis.

The fundamental question is, "Whom are we treating — a patient with a disease or a disease which happens to be in a patient?"

Will our answers be found in WHAT we do, or rather HOW we approach it and WHY we do it? And will it not ultimately be the same for the patient when it comes to healing?

A growing need for an integrative approach to health encompassing the full understanding and commitment of the patient in their course of therapy is evident. Treating a "disease" without treating the person who developed it is pointless. The advantages of engaging patients as co-facilitators in achieving improved health far outweigh the biomedical "GP as Expert" approach. What's more, research shows the patient's increased control over their body and health yields beneficial results.

So as a doctor, what extent of responsibility do you have in assessing the situation and exploring the "prescriptions" possible? How much of the patient's story will you relate to and what are the filters through which you will assess the choices they are making and the possible impact those choices have on their lives? Stepping away from the simple drug prescription associated with the said diagnosis, the role the doctor plays must necessarily change.

When one delves into the root causes of diseases, etiology, circumstances, aggravating factors, stressors, coping skills, psychological outlook, support systems available … etc., the prescription becomes much more elaborate and individualized. What is true for one patient suffering from the same disease or ailment is not necessarily true for another.

Plan for Mind-Body-Matrix-Spirit

"If a feeling becomes strong enough, it might become an image. This image can be of help for the mind."
T.S. Elliot

Each patient's prescribed course of treatment will vary based on their individual condition and circumstances; however, every prescription can be enhanced by addressing the emotional, as well as the physical aspects of a patient's situation.

Overall, mind-body medicine reduces stress and enhances well-being. According to Ernst, mind-body medicine has been shown to reduce stress and enhance well-being, regardless of the specific condition and symptoms. He says, "These mind-body techniques help change the way individuals think about the problem, which gives them more control over their responses to the stress.

"This enables individuals to manage and even reduce their stress because they are able to assert control over their reactions and behaviors to the stress... It is not the stress itself that causes physical and mental harm, but it is the reaction to the stress that determines how the individual experiences it. It becomes essential for individuals to learn how to control their thoughts, attitudes, and behaviors when encountering stressful situations." (Ernst, 2001)

Furthermore, direct patient involvement in the healing process, such as with self-regulatory intervention methods, has shown beneficial effects. An illustration of this is the research paper by S. E. Sauer et al. (2010) who explored the use of self-regulation theory for understanding and treating chronic pain in patients with temporomandibular disorders (TMD).

The authors concluded that, "With focused efforts to increase self-regulatory strength and alter the physiological deregulation common among chronic TMD patients, PSR (patient self-regulation) may be seen as an integrative treatment approach that warrants further consideration in the management of chronic pain. Treatment approaches like PSR that serve to better regulate the ANS (autonomic nervous system) through enhanced self-regulatory capacity provide a streamlined way of addressing the equally important physical and psychological components of the chronic pain experience." (Sauer et.al. 2010, p 812)

The Relaxation Response

Patient management of their own stress level through the relaxation response, pioneered in 1976 by Herbert Benson, M.D., head of the Mind/Body Medical Institute at New England Deaconess Hospital and Harvard Medical School, Division of Behavioral Medicine, offers further evidence of the benefits of involving patients in their treatment.

Dr. Benson explains in his book *The Relaxation Response* that physiological changes occur in an individual who partakes in this therapy and engages in a repetitive mental activity while consciously ignoring negative distracting thoughts.

Decreased heart rate, rapid decrease in blood lactate associated with lower levels of anxiety, and reduced blood pressure in persons with hypertension occur during the relaxation response, as demonstrated by Dr. Benson. "Alpha brain waves, associated with feelings of well-being and relaxation, increase in frequency and intensity. These physical changes are a sign of decreased activity of the sympathetic nervous system, indicating a sense of calmness and low anxiety. The relaxation response gives individuals control over their physiological actions, giving them generalized self-control and peace." (Benson, 1975)

Experiencing the relaxation response is one of the highlights of the BowenFirst™ therapy, and perhaps a key foundation of its success. Within minutes of the treatment, patients enter the relaxation response, so that when the specific procedures are performed, the patient is highly disposed to receive the therapeutic benefits. Healing takes place when the body is in a parasympathetic state, and as such, other therapies like hypnosis and imagery therapy have had some preliminary success at establishing the positive physiological effects experienced.

"Outcomes of using imagery for relaxation include increased oxygen saturation levels, lower blood pressure, lower heart rate, warmer extremities, reduced muscle tension, greater alpha waves on EEG, and expression of sensing less or no anxiety overall," according to researchers Post-White and Fitzgerald in Complementary/Alternative Theories in Nursing (2002). "Eliminating negative responses and formulating positive images helps reduce the physiologic stress response of the body," continue Post-White and Fitzgerald.

What's more, techniques such as humor can be very effective in relaxing patients, allowing them to better handle any fear and anxiety. In fact, "Nurses find humor to be very beneficial for increasing their patients' pain threshold, which helps them relax and reduce their stress," writes K. Smith in Complementary/Alternative Theories in Nursing (2002).

Given the research in psychoneuroimmunology showing the importance of stress and the effects it has on the body, and the findings in the pain research showing coping skills to be the most useful approach to diminishing the impact of stress, it is apparent that approaches that focus on "stress" play an important part in the health of patients. This is really the paradigm in which it becomes impossible to separate the body from the mind.

The underlying etiology of many major medical problems, such as coronary disease, accidents, suicides, and depression, is stress and its effects on the body. Many of these conditions are preventable in part or in total, and research shows integrating mind-body techniques with conventional medical practice appears to be of significant relevance (Pelletier, 2002). The growing number of individuals and health care professionals using mind-body medicine attests to its positive impact on the health and well-being of individuals.

We really are at a crossroads where we have the choice to try and understand what the effect of these "alternative" or "complementary" approaches have to offer to the whole patient and see whether it actually takes the concerted effort and intention of the patient to surmount his or her symptoms or whether more research on the biological model will bring about the solutions. Of course, there is no harm in following both paths but it is paramount to create proper research protocols to effectively evaluate the impact of "holistic" therapies.

Stress Causes Cancer

In a study funded by The National Institute on Aging (NIA) and the National Cancer Institute (NCI), researchers interviewed 94 women whose breast cancer had spread (metastatic) or returned (recurrent) about the stress in their lives. David Spiegel, M.D., one of the study's authors and a faculty member at the Stanford University School of Medicine, found there were marked differences among women who had experienced different levels of stress.

"Comparisons revealed a significantly longer disease-free interval among women reporting no traumatic or stressful life events," says Dr. Spiegel. A history of traumatic events early in life can have many physical and emotional effects, including changing the hormonal stress response system.

Dealing with Traumatic Stress Directly

Even more significant is what Dr. Spiegel refers to as "good news." "Our research has shown that people do better in the aftermath of traumatic stress if they deal with it directly. Facing it rather than fleeing is important. We have conducted support groups for more than 30 years, and found that dealing with traumatic and very stressful experiences is much healthier. In other words, don't suppress your emotions" (Spiegel, 2008).

This research indicates that emotional support, community, and the ability to share actually impact biological results. So why does so much "research" focus on biological approaches to cancer treatment, when clearly a holistic, or at least an integrative approach is more likely to be effective? My clinical experience certainly concurs with the research, and moreover, when I see patients "cured" of cancer but not liberated from the emotionally draining circumstances, it is evident to me that they know they are not out of the danger zone.

Researchers have long questioned why some people are resilient to stress while others aren't. Dr. Eric J. Nestler of the University of Texas Southwestern Medical Center examined the biology behind stress resilience. His study investigated the vulnerability of mice to stress after social defeat. When mice are put in cages with bigger, more aggressive mice, some still avoid social interactions with other mice even a month later—a sign that the stress has overwhelmed them. Some, however, adapt and continue to interact.

This research, funded by NIH's National Institute of

Mental Health (NIMH), found that the mice, which do not recover from stress have higher rates of nerve cell electrical activity in the cells that make dopamine, a chemical that helps transmit nerve impulses. More nerve cell electrical activity caused the subject mice to make more of a protein (BDNF), which has been linked to a susceptibility to stress.

Dr. Nestler concludes from the research that, "The fact that we could increase these animals' ability to adapt to stress by blocking BDNF and its signals means that it may be possible to develop compounds that improve our own resilience to stress. This is a great opportunity to explore how to increase resistance in situations that might otherwise result in post-traumatic stress disorder."(Nestler, 2008)

The Jungle Prescription Ayahuasca

Reflecting on this commentary, two points come to mind. On the one hand, we can explore "compounds" that block the nerve cell electrical activity causing increased BDNF, or we can find therapies that may decrease the electrical activities or increase receptor sites for dopamine. One such natural therapy is explored in the documentary "Jungle Prescription," about an Amazonian plant called ayahuasca, known as the "vine of the souls." There are many other therapeutic approaches that can have an impact on our physiology as well. On the other hand, given that we are not mice in cages, maybe it is time to re-evaluate the type of lives we lead and the choices that we make which are responsible for eliciting such a reaction.

Maybe it is time to make radical choices, not only in learning to better manage our choices, but also in making choices in our lifestyles that are more health-sustainable. There is no magic pill to clean up our health, our environment and our lives without first clearly establishing the values we hold and being accountable for the choices we are making.

As the previous research on recurring breast cancer seems to indicate, it is not the stress itself that determines the disease outcomes, but how the stress is dealt with in its immediate aftermath that determines the rate of recovery. If support groups play such an instrumental part in the recovery, then it seems evident that a purely biological approach would be fraught with limitations.

Prescribing Empowerment

So as a doctor, what extent of responsibility do you have in assessing the situation and exploring the "pre-scriptions" possible? How much of the patient's story will you relate to, and what are the filters through which you will be assessing the choices they are making and the possible impact it is having on their lives?

When one steps away from the simple drug prescription associated with the said diagnosis, the role the doctor plays must necessarily change. When one delves in the root causes of diseases, etiology, circumstances, aggravating factors, stressors, coping skills, psychological outlook, support systems available, etc. the prescription becomes much more elaborate and individualized. What is true for one patient suffering from the same disease or ailment is not necessarily true for the other.

One of the most effective ways of helping the patient to take the steps that will help him or her gain their health back is to have them share the "meaning" of their symptoms. Implicit in the self-diagnosis is the solution. It has been my experience that patients by and large know what their problem is, how they got there, and when given different options, know what course of treatment will most likely help them.

An interesting development taking place in some of the research is assessing the impact of the theory that the body is the "carrier of meaning" and thus has a history. This educational approach is inspired by the "personal construct theory" of Kelly (1955) and Nygard's (1993) use of the theory within the field of human understanding. When a patient is able to gather meaning and attribute an understanding to their health status, this enhanced awareness is a high motivator to participate in improving their health.

The work of Steen et al., Generalized chronic musculoskeletal pain as a rational reaction to a life situation— explores the perspective that the "body" with chronic musculoskeletal pain is seen as a carrier of meaning. "Helping a person with chronic pain to become aware of knowledge embedded in the body, and letting her/him make interpretations of the pain, might also challenge both the traditional health expert role and patient role." (Steen et al. 2011) This approach poses both epistemological and methodological challenges and clearly necessitates a review of the patient-doctor relationship.

"The theoretical implications of the scholarly discovery

that the body has a history, and is as much a cultural phenomenon as it is a biological entity, are potentially enormous. Also, if indeed the body is passing through a critical historical moment, this moment also offers a critical methodological opportunity to reformulate theories of culture, self and experience, with the body at the centre of analysis." (Chordas, T. 1996, p.4)

When a patient is able to gather meaning and attribute an understanding to their health status, this enhanced awareness is a high motivator to participate in their health reconstruction and improvement. Bannister and Fransella state that "methods to enhance reconstruction, and thus new meanings, range from those of the artist to those of the scientist, and that many techniques for achieving these kinds of changes have not yet been invented." (Bannister and Fransella, 1986, pp.117-133)

Researchers concur that what is needed is methodology that allows the person to elaborate on his personal meanings of events and the possibilities of alternative constructions.

A Shift in Perspective

Finding ways for patients to shift their perspectives, "… to create opportunities for the group participants to make a shift in personal insights from the body as object to the body as a ''talking subject," may be one of the most powerful prescriptions for health. Thus, "Awareness of possible connections between thoughts, feelings and bodily reactions in various situations and social relations (was found to be) therefore essential." (Merleau-Ponty, 1996)

When a person starts to comprehend her/his experience

in terms of a metaphor, they find the power to create a new reality. "If a new metaphor enters the conceptual system that we base our actions on, it will alter that conceptual system and the perceptions and actions that the system gives rise to," write Lakoff & Johnson (1981). Clearly the approach of "reading" the messages of the body has clinically important results for the management of pain. Giving the patient tools that can engage and encourage their ability to read the messages of their body helps them recover faster.

With my own patients, I share with them that the low back pain they are experiencing may be associated with the kidney. I explain to them that in Chinese medicine, the kidneys are associated with the emotion of fear. In cases where back pain may have elicited fear resulting from fearful circumstances, this knowledge appears to reassure the patient. It is as if they are able to make more sense of their symptoms, and thus when I perform the work, the patient's attention is on addressing the fear, and they feel that the fear is being addressed.

The correlation of the body part with the emotional memory of the fear establishes a deeper connection and acknowledges the fear. Making explicit the mind-body connection plays an integral role in the ability to release the traumatic element stored in the tissues of the body, and can enhance healing.

An excellent example of this phenomenon is the patient who has been in a motor vehicle accident. Those who take the route of pain medication to alleviate their symptoms are very likely to end up in the chronic pain cycle, as the symptom of "pain" is the only part of the problem being addressed. They are disempowered and the pain meds often cover-up the issues in the tissues that require addressing and healing for full recovery to take place.

If the trauma has not left their body, those who take the route of physiotherapy and attempt to rehabilitate their muscles will typically get 20% to 30% improvement without ever feeling free from the accident.

The motor vehicle accident patients I treat typically improve very quickly because of several factors. First, the treatment itself is done when the body enters the relaxation response. In addition, the specific procedures are performed to address the shock stored in the body, with the patient cognizant of this information. When the accident "took their breath away" or they were "aghast" or "winded," restoring proper breathing patterns and full use of their lungs and proper tension of their diaphragm is paramount prior to addressing their whiplash, for example.

Addressing the trauma first will result in just a few treatments needed to address the whiplash. In contrast, merely treating the neck without treating the person who experienced the whiplash could take years and may never really produce satisfactory results. Furthermore, the treatment restores the fascia, decreases inflammatory responses, and increases circulation, lymphatic flow and overall vitality to the patient.

Tricking the Brain

I have also observed a connection between the two sides of the body. When there is injury to one side of the body, treating the side or limb that has not been affected is more effective. Performing the same moves on the limb that would not perceive a pain sensation seemingly "tricks" the brain into not perceiving any pain sensations when the painful or affected side is worked on. As the patient's body integrates the procedure, the brain appears to have been trained to optimize healing.

The Science of Pain

Just how can patients train their brain, and what should we know about this process?

Neurophysiology studies confirm that pain changes neuronal activity and anatomical connectivity in multiple areas of the brain, particularly in the areas of cognition and emotional assessment.

Acute tissue damage causing pain triggers changes in the central nervous system (CNS) that contribute to the development of secondary hyperalgesia and associated sensory disturbances. Yet within eight days, reversible CNS changes are measurable in healthy individuals who suffer from repetitive painful stimuli. This cortical reorganization showing measurable CNS changes have been linked to lower pain thresholds and hypersensitivity and may play a role in the development of chronic pain.

This reorganization of structural and functional connectivity in the neurons, or "plasticity", is strongly activity-dependent. Negative psychological sequelae, such as fear avoidance and the symptoms of acute post-traumatic stress, are likely to impede functional recovery via these feedback pathways. In a recent study by Edgar, Dale et al. (2011), the authors proposed a cortical retraining program that could benefit burn patients by directing conscious attention to and normalizing sensation of the injured limb as pain-free.

Phantom Limb Pain

Several studies illustrate the powerful effect of the brain on healing. A 2011 study established neural evidence for the brain's role in controlling motor output. (Tanaka et al., 2011, p.38) As physical fatigue signals are fed back to the brain through sensory systems, and the brain controls motor output to maintain physical performance and homeostasis, "the mirror visual feedback system may also influence the fatigue-related changes in the motor cortex."

This finding confirms the work of Ramachandran et al. (1995) on visual feedback using Ramachandran's mirror box to treat semi-paresis following stroke and phantom limb pain. The authors establish that multimodal sensory information, especially visual information; contribute to the integration of sensorimotor loops and consequently internal representations of movement.

Said in another way, it is through the eyes that we see an action, which we can repeat in our minds until such time that our brain can repeat and potentiate the action.

Ramachandran's earlier studies employed concurrent

imagery of phantom hand movement; however, more recent studies show that "movement and stimulation of one hand also transfer to the other hand" and are in accordance with the findings of Brodie et al. (2007) that "mere movement of the intact hand without a mirror also led to a change in phantom pain and phantom sensation."

Yet another study demonstrated that viewing movements of one's hand in a mirror evoked "activity in the brain contralateral to the hand that is perceived." (Diers, Martin et al., 2010) Thus, the brain feels what it perceives, rather than the actual physical stimulus.

Knowing this, and considering that intention is registered through brain activity, we have discovered that our therapeutic treatments which lack research may well be onto something that can be neurologically explained. It always baffles me when treating one leg, the other one responds, whether I have touched it or not. Numerous patients have shared that while working on their "good" knee, the injured knee experiences sensations of tingling or a flush of heat, which they interpret as, increased circulation. Once again this is also an example of the patient's mindful participation in their treatment, which we know is a significant contributor to their recovery.

Due in part to the discovery of the neurophysiological "mirror" neurons, which discharge not only during action execution, but also action observation; research is postulating that these neurons are the substrate for action understanding. (Kilner et al., 2007)

This query brings up the nature of intention and

the ability to "understand" or "copy" the intention of another through observation. Since social interaction depends upon our ability to infer beliefs and intentions in others, a motor rendition of a visually learned observation assumes an intention to the observed movement. "The intention that is inferred from the observation of the action now depends upon the prior information received from a context level… The Mirror Neuron System (MNS) believes the reason for the observed movement is to 'cure'."(Kilner, 2007)

Therefore, the MNS is capable of inferring a unique intention, even if two intentions result in identical movements. This observation is supported empirically. Mirror neurons in the cortical area of the parietal frontal lobule, or PF, have been shown to have differential patterns of firing when viewing movements that are virtually identical at the kinematic level, but differ at the level of intention. (Kilner, 2007)

Thus, it appears that direct patient involvement in the process of healing, established through their own interpretation of the meaning of their symptomatology, as well as a clear visual formulation of their intention to potentiate a healing action, is a "prescription" that will yield the best results. The doctor's role is to help educate and support the process.

Prescribing Pills

In contrast to the more empowered approach of viewing a patient's pain as "one of their symptoms," a pathophysiological approach to pain focuses on pain relief as the primary objective. The choice of intervention is usually pharmaceutical.

The pain experience is one of the most challenging to find the root of. It is nearly impossible to separate the individual factors that are in play both in the existing research on pain and in the clinical experience of patients in pain.

Expectations and verbal suggestions appear to significantly affect the experience of the prescribed treatment, according to recent research. Several studies show that verbal suggestions can induce high pain expectations, with patients reporting significantly more pain than subjects who received verbal suggestions inducing low pain expectations. (Arntz & Claassens, 2004; Benedetti et al., 2007; Colloca et al., 2008; Staats et al., 1998) Furthermore, research demonstrates that expectations about pain can alter central pain modulation. (Flaten et al., 1999; Benedetti et al., 2007; Goffaux et al., 2009; Van Laarhoven et al., 2010)

Mindfulness and The Perception of Pain

This means that we do have some direct control over our biological process. In fact our mindfulness of the process can actually affect the way we perceive pain. Several research studies have established that expectations of pain actually influence pain perception (Benedetti et al., 2003; Flaten et al., 2006; Kirsch, 1999; Price et al., 1999; Wager, 2005). Strong correlations between expected and experienced pain have also been reported. (Montgomery & Kirsch, 1997)

This realization of the results of our mindful

intention and intervention has its corollary opposite, in that negative thoughts produce negative results. "The perception of different ambiguous stimuli can be influenced by negative suggestions in such a way that negative expectations can adversely influence the intensity of itch or pain experienced" concluded researchers studying the effects of nocebo and placebo. (Laarhoven, et al., 2011, p.1493)

"Despite the widespread prevalence of regional musculoskeletal pain conditions, little has been published on their effective pharmacological management," according to Milton Cohen, of the Department of Rheumatology, in New South Wales. "Inadequate understanding of pathogenesis, difficulties with nosology, and the variable response of these conditions to a variety of treatment modalities have been factors confounding the assessment of therapeutic agents." (Sheather-Reid, R.B. et. al. 1998, pp244-252)

The Placebo Effect

In his study on efficacy of pain relief agents, the agents used were opioids and non-opioid analgesics (such as nonsteroidal anti-inflammatory drugs (NSAIDs) and acetaminophen (paracetamol)) to examine the analgesic efficacy of the opioid agonist codeine versus the nonsteroidal anti-inflammatory drug ibuprofen in regional cervicobrachial pain using N-of–1 methodology. Analgesic effect was monitored by patient self-report of clinical effect. The study showed that there was no statistically significant difference between patients who used analgesics and those who took a placebo.

Similar results were reported in another study on N-of-1 methodology in 19 subjects (U.S. Cancer Pain Relief Committee, 1998) with neuropathic pain in which "no significant differences (were found) between placebo and dextromethorphan for any of the outcome measures, leading to the conclusion that dextromethorphan was ineffective in neuropathic pain." (Sheather-Reid,1998)

Other studies point out that the variable effects of analgesia are dependent on the way it was administered. For example, experiments have shown that a given dose of morphine relieves post-surgical pain to a considerably greater extent when administered openly in a standard injection procedure, than when administered in a hidden fashion by means of a computerized infusion pump, without the patient knowing when it will be given. (Colloca et al., 2005, pp.545–552)

In addition, research shows that the placebo effect can be greatly increased if the patient's expectations of the results are increased. For example, telling a patient in pain that he is about to receive a powerful painkiller can either produce or enhance analgesic responses. Abundant experimental evidence demonstrates that research subjects often experience substantial analgesic responses when they are administered a pain stimulus and then given an inert placebo intervention deceptively described as a powerful pain-relieving agent. (Colloca et al., 2005)

Why all these variable results? If drugs are supposed to have a predictable result on certain pathways or for certain diseases, then how can we get such variable results?

The reality is that the "non-scientific" component in the equation is actually the "subject" of the experiment—the patient.

"Scientific assessment of benefits from symptomatic treatments, such as analgesic agents, has been based on the assumption that treatment interventions will produce predictable benefits in patients with a given condition that can be measured in aggregate statistics derived from randomized clinical trials and extrapolated to clinical practice. However, placebo and nocebo research reveals that the context in which symptomatic treatments are provided, and notably the information communicated to patients, creates expectations that influence the observed outcomes in terms of which benefits and risks are defined."(Colloca et al., 2005 p.237)

The problem is several-fold. When reviewing research on drug efficacy deemed appropriate to address certain diagnosed conditions, we find that many drugs are withdrawn and do not even make it to FDA approval due to their side effects. Many drugs on the market (as it only take a statistically marginal "benefit" in the trial to move up the eligibility ladder) have only marginally better results than placebo alone. Furthermore, research now shows that their effectiveness is determined by the context in which they are given, and the expectations of the patient.

So if it's not the disease we are fooling, is it the patient? If so many drugs are statistically insignificant in their results, can we do better than a placebo or at least make the most of the placebo effect?

Professor Maureen Simmonds, of Texas Woman's University, Department of Physical Therapy, while reviewing the history of the term placebo and its usage in medicine, argues that since traditional health care is primarily based on physiology and pathophysiology, treatments are developed and targeted using a physiological approach. It is therefore not surprising that this framework is used to explain specific treatment effects.

"In this context, non-physiological or placebo effects of treatment are regarded as artifacts. However, this simple categorization of physiological versus non-physiological effects is an oversimplification"(Simmonds, 2000).

The "use of a single term (placebo) to describe disparate phenomena is potentially misleading because it creates a spurious impression of homogeneity and stability of response," argues Richardson (1989) "It is now evident that this non-physiologic 'noise' has physiological effects." (Hashish et al., 1988; Simmonds, 2000)

Scientist Herbert Benson notes there are three components necessary for the placebo effect to take place:

- The belief and expectation of the patient;
- The belief and expectation of the doctor;
- The doctor-patient relationship.

When it comes to using a placebo, does the end justify the means? Some would argue that deliberately giving a patient something that we know does not work is misleading, whereas giving something we believe would benefit the patient because of the placebo effect is ethical. What really determines the answer here is whether helping or serving the patient is paramount.

I do not intend to debate this issue here, for the issues are already well described. (see Miller, 2001)Consider the fact that as NDs, "Do no Harm" is a fundamental tenet of our practice. Everything else aside, if the results are similar whether or not we prescribe drugs, by not prescribing we at least would be sparing the patient from the side effects often associated with drug use.

If the benefit to the patient is really the primary issue,

then we could even explore practices that claim to have high case study empirical success and analyze whether there is merit for the modality used in and of itself, or whether it was just the context of the practitioner-patient relationship that was able to create a placebo effect.

As Simmonds points out, "… conditioning appears to be complemented by expectancies, and it is difficult to tease out the relative contributions of each. Placebo effects are influenced by context and suggestion, as well as by the conditioning effect of a specific treatment." (Price, 1999)

Unfortunately, any treatment that is not well understood but which works gets grouped into the simple explanation that it was "just the placebo" effect, when research investigating the reasons for positive therapeutic incomes is really called for.

I am not advocating that natural therapies not be subject to the same statistical standards as drug therapies. However, do we really understand the mechanisms and the factors involved in the placebo effect, and what specific influences the doctor-patient relationship, as well the patient's mindset have on the treatment outcome?

Viewing the "placebo" as the trigger to a self-generated and "supported" (i.e. doctor-facilitated) initiative of the patient to take charge and get better, what is the next step on the path which doesn't lead to a self-effacing and disempowered feeling, and possibly to a nocebo effect, when the patient finds out that they got better on "nothing?" The reality is that there is still "research" which "prove" homeopathy to be purely placebo and such research has the potential of negatively influencing the progress of the patient. Not because homeopathy is invalid, but because the trust between the patient and doctor risks being breached. When one looks at such research, it is evident that the criteria was inadequate— for example giving the same remedy based on a condition rather than the patient for example. None the less, so called scientific research is held in high esteem even though the continual evolution of parameters for research widens the debate and continually disproved prior held findings.

For others, getting better on "nothing" means they had "nothing" to begin with, and that it was all in their head. The problem with that interpretation of the process is evident. Placebo is not "nothing," when the fact is that the process of taking the "placebo" empowers the body with the necessary tools to start the healing process since the body is already primed for self-healing.

The "Positivo Effect"

If we redefine the "placebo effect" as the "aligned and committed effect," or the "positivo effect," then we have no preconceived negatives to fall back on. We are, in essence, setting the stage for specific goals and outcomes by providing daily routines to reinforce them. We also provide inspiration and hope, but with direction, goals and specificity. What if the "aligned and committed effect" was in operation while the patients received effective treatment free from negative side effects?

"Rather than writing off non-allopathic processes, the scientific community is indicating to the medical community that the thoughts and emotions of the patient can be in and of themselves enough to generate good health. With this in mind, all methods of complementary health can be looked at with a different and more open viewpoint. While some modalities certainly appear to have no scientific or logical reason for their success, it is too easy to condemn them as fringe or charlatan practices without research." (Quinlan, 2011)

Furthermore, research keeps unveiling new mechanisms of action which were previously unknown such as in July 2014, The University of Singapore explored the possibility of dysfunction in one or more components of the pain Neuromatrix to provide evidence of altered neural connectivity and activation in patients with low back pain and irritable bowel syndrome who had apparent absence of injury or disease. The point is that if these patients get better with a treatment who's mechanism is also not fully understood, maybe the treatment is working on the aspects that science has not yet discovered or fully understood such as the pain neuromatrix. The net result is what happens for the patient. If they improve, then something positive has been achieved.

Although the Cartesian approach to medicine has made amazing advances, it ignores the possibility of capitalizing on the patient's emotional and spiritual well-being from a humanistic approach. We are entering an age in health care where patients are looking for customized and individualized treatment in which they feel they are co-creators of their wellness. Furthermore, research keeps unveiling new mechanisms of action which were previously unknown such as in July 2014, The University of Singapore explored the possibility of dysfunction in one or more components of the pain Neuromatrix to provide evidence of altered neural connectivity and activation in patients with low back pain and irritable bowel syndrome who had apparent absence of injury or disease. The point is that if these patients get better with a treatment who's mechanism is also not fully understood, maybe the treatment is working on the aspects that science has not yet discovered or fully understood such as the pain Neuromatrix. The net result is what happens for the patient. If they improve, then something positive has been achieved.

As research would have it, some doctors now believe that the placebo effect is due to a response within the mind and body that strengthens the immune system and speeds healing. (Thornton, 1993) Is that not the principle behind psychoneuroimmunology? And doesn't it confirm that commitment and clear goals should always be the first steps in the healing process?

Is there something that has yet to be better understood that takes place when a patient engages in a course of treatment? According to Milton Cohen, when considering pain there is, "The self-referentiality of living systems (through their qualities of autopoiesis, noncentrality and negentropy) sees pain 'emerge' in unpredictable ways that defy any lineal reduction of the lived experience to any particular 'thing.'

"Pain therefore constitutes an aporia, a space and presence that denies us access to its secrets. We suggest a project in which pain may be apprehended in the clinical encounter, through the engagement of two autonomous, self-referential beings in the inter subjective or so-called third space, from which new therapeutic possibilities can arise." (Cohen, 2008,pp. 824–834)

Aligning Emotional Energy to Treatment

What seems to be true in my practice is that if patients are aligned with their choice of treatment, they will engage their mental and emotional energy and commit to its success. Trying to suggest a treatment that is not aligned will not create the same results.

In a recent article the authors explore the neglected

connection between risk benefit assessment and informed consent in which the information communicated to patients can influence treatment benefits and risks. They argue that information disclosure has potentially powerful positive and negative influences on health outcomes, and then analyze a study in which they conclude that the "placebo effect" was greater when the patients were positively aligned with the procedure, rather than in the study in which there was uncertainty on whether or not they would get the procedure done. (Franklin et al., 2001)

In the following study on vertebroplasty and the relevance of patient disclosure, it was shown that patient disclosure does have an impact on results as it influences expectations. In the first study there was no patient disclosure and the results were attributed to the placebo effect. In the second study where there was disclosure, patients did not know whether they were receiving the "treatment" or were receiving a "sham treatment." But there was too much uncertainty to align themselves with the positive expected results and clinically they did not do as well.

"To further illustrate the impact of information disclosure on treatment benefits, consider the widely-used treatment for painful vertebral fractures known as vertebroplasty (which involves injecting cement into the spine with the aim of relieving pain by stabilizing the fracture). In 2009, the New England Journal of Medicine published the results of two double-blind sham-controlled trials, which demonstrated no difference in pain relief between vertebroplasty and a fake invasive intervention without injecting cement.

"In contrast, a more recent unblinded randomized trial comparing vertebroplasty to conservative medical therapy demonstrated substantially greater improvement in pain. A reasonable interpretation of these two sets of trials is that vertebroplasty is effective in relieving pain, not as the result of injecting cement but by virtue of the placebo response."

"The power of information disclosure to influence patient outcomes is borne out by the fact that patients receiving vertebroplasty in the sham-controlled trials (Buchbinder et al., 2009; Kallmes et al., 2009) reported a substantially lower mean reduction in pain as compared with similar patients who received vertebroplasty in the open trial of this procedure. … In the former, they knew as a result of the informed consent disclosure that they had a 50% chance of receiving either vertebroplasty or a fake intervention disguised as the real procedure. In the latter, they knew that they were receiving standard vertebroplasty.

"These results suggest that patients' expectations of benefits were diminished in the sham-controlled trials compared to the open trial, as a result of being informed about the double-blind study design and thus being uncertain about whether they were receiving a real treatment believed by practitioners to be beneficial, or a fake treatment provided as a control intervention." (Buchbinder et al., 2009; Kallmes et al., 2009; Klazen et al., 2010)

This is a clear case in point that often it is the commitment and alignment to what one feels is right that makes the difference, not the actual procedure, treatment or medication taken as they are by necessity part and parcel of the context."

As we have seen, there is an increased therapeutic effect if the patient is aligned with the treatment and receives positive reinforcement of the outcomes. Research also supports the notion that the patient's increased control over their health and body has beneficial effects. Treatments that encourage patient empowerment and share tools for better control of reactions to stress act to favorably reinforce the direction of patients' health outcomes and are worthy of consideration in the treatment "Plan."

Are You The Healer in Your Household?

In the previous section, I addressed the role of the doctor. In this section, I want to directly address you, the patient. I firmly believe that the more you bring to the table, the more profound your health will be improved. It may take some time to identify a doctor with whom you can create this partnership, but the good news is that there is plenty you can do, starting right now.

In this section I will expand upon some of the patient stories I shared in the "Subjective" section of the book, demonstrating the possibility of different outcomes, and the kind of observation process you can start to apply to your current situation. My goal is to raise questions to get you started in better understanding your relationship to your symptoms and get clearer on your health objectives by illustrating key principles of the "Listen process" at work. I have developed a full program called the LISTEN Principles, which is intended to guide you through this process step by step. I will be sharing this with you as we refer back to some of the patients' stories.

The 67-year-old women with the patella fracture.

What if the patient with the simple fracture had been interviewed differently at the time of her injury? What if the trauma she experienced had been identified?

What if the discussion of differing opinions with regard to immobilization had been part of the information shared with her? These are the kinds of therapeutic questions that the LISTEN Principles allows us to raise. Let's explore this approach with this patient and the benefits which may have come from this process.

In her after care, she was told to try not moving the limb and to keep it elevated. What if her imagination ran wild and she believed that she could snap at the knee and separate the bony sutures? Her mind worked on keeping her leg stiff and still, so that no further breaks would occur. No one checked in on her assumptions or suggested that she work with her body. She was afraid of her body and what it could do to her.

What if the physiotherapy team had addressed her "solidifying impression of stiffness" by informing her that gentle movement would bring circulation to the area and speed up the healing process? The point is that she lacked information and she never questioned her assumptions. She took what she thought was true and let her mind be carried away with thoughts based on her fear.

Then, when home care was arranged, this patient encountered a different physiotherapist with a different point of view. She told her that movement was good and that pain was good. She was advised to keep moving and bending the knee, so that it would become less stiff, "She had to move it even if it caused pain."

This patient went from fearing movement and keeping stiff to "hurting herself" with movement to get her knee limber. Her underlining feeling was that her knee was like a "foreign object", a force to be contended with: first feared, then conquered.

She found herself confused and worried that she may have done something wrong by listening to the first advice. Her anxiety grew. Her healing was slow, much slower than was normally anticipated. By two months, she had more pain, less mobility and felt that she had failed. She felt the victim of her situation.

What if you were this patient? Would you have suffered the same outcome? What would you have done differently? What if, instead, you had access to the information on how joints heal? What if you were given a clear perspective on risk factors for re-injury? What if you had been taught to observe your words: e.g., the use of "stiff", "paralyzed with fear", and "immobile"?

The point is that we must take the responsibility to get informed. This may require consulting with different people, or searching the Internet so that we can ask the right questions. The truth is that there is so much information that it is impossible for doctors to stay abreast of all the latest discoveries and theories. Information is key, but for information to be meaningful, it must feel relevant to your experience.

No perspective is ever objective. It's always limited by our personal experience and knowledge. This is where it is really important to be able to self-reflect, attribute a health goal, a.k.a. "objective" and consider what you are willing to experience in order to get there.

This patient feared that she could not look after herself, that she might be dependent on others. What if this fear was addressed? She perceived her fall as representing a fast decline into "old age." What if that thought had been challenged and someone had taken the time to explain that this is not an "old age" injury? What if her confusion that the break was caused by osteoporosis were addressed? And what if it were reframed by explaining that had she fallen on her hip, as she first claimed, her bones were probably not osteoporotic or she would have had a hip fracture?

What this patient really needed was to address the psychological trauma in this incident. Of course, she shared her fears and trauma in the interview with her doctor and attending nurse but it never was considered in the "Plan" stage of the SOAP form. Her diagnosis was a broken patella and her Plan was surgery and a prescription for pain.

What if she could have brought motion and subtleness to the area and asked her body what it wanted? What if she had known the powerful effects of visualization? What if she could have healed with trust and self-love and not lived in fear? Her healing process would have been much faster and she would have suffered much less pain.

The point is that had she learned to Inquire and work with her body, her fate would have been different.

Following are a list of questions that can help you look at a health issue and more quickly determine what is more aligned with your own objectives.

Questions to ask yourself:

- Do I have all the information I need on the healing process?

- Do I have the knowledge necessary to form an opinion?
- Do I know how to gauge improvement and assess the choice I have made?
- What is my body saying?
- What does my body need?
- Am I viewing my body as the culprit?
- Am I willing to work with my body?
- What language am I using to describe my injured body? Is it reinforcing malfunction or healing?
- Do I trust the process I have chosen?

Before becoming comfortable with a decision, it must be aligned with your core values about health. For this you need to start with information but you must also contextualize this information. Furthermore, you must develop insight on where you stand in the spectrum of fear to love. Are you reacting to fear? How can you tell? I use the term "chaotic vibration" in my LISTEN program to help identify from what level we are operating. If we are not at ease, and operate from fear, we can learn to identify it. Here is a sample of the information I cover in the L in Listen Principles:

L: Love—healing is about listening to and loving your body

- Discover how you eliminate chaotic vibration in your body.
- Ensure you are not operating at counter purposes
- Establish whether you are fighting your body
- Determine whether your eating habits are nourishing your body, feeding your ulcer, or stuffing your guts.
- Determine on a scale from 1 to 10 how much fear governs your life.

The female patient with childhood polio

What if, in the case of the patient with polio, who could not achieve proper gait, she had help in reframing her perspective? What if she were able to be more accepting of her body? This same acceptance would allow her to meet the men behind their "improper demeanor." Maybe all she could see was their physical challenges, which she was unwilling to see another way. Accepting her body could have given her the confidence to meet the person behind the men that she perceived as undesirable? Indeed, once she really met them, she may have discovered they too were complete multifaceted human beings not defined by their physical challenges. Her own body-image and self-consciousness blinded her to this possibility.

Her version of the body, starting with her own, was probably based on a stereotypical perfection. This was apparent in how her hair was put together: impeccably styled to frame her face and prevent any escaping strands from accentuating her delicate nose, set between her perfectly symmetrical eyes. When questioned a bit, which of course I cannot help myself to do, her eyes gazed downward, not as in shame, but with a type of haughtiness, perceptible in her slightly raised chin and her pursed lips, as if saying, "I am not prepared to go there, just fix my legs."

From the therapeutic perspective, it is in the subjective experience of her disease and her underlining assumptions, not in in the objective findings, that the true assessment and prescriptions are found. Therefore, until she is open to look at her assumptions, there is little room for recovery.

This inward looking can, of course, be done under therapeutic guidance, but the good news is that it is also a process that can be done on one's own. When I originally wrote this book, I had not completed the guided program for patients that would serve this exact need.

Here are some questions that might have helped this patient if she had been open to the possibility of a deeper healing:

- Am I making excuses for my life?
- Am I blaming a part of me to justify my unhappiness?
- Will I only be happy when…..?
- Is what I don't accept in others a reflection of what I don't accept in myself?
- Can I see that when I am able to love myself, with all my "imperfections," only then can I fully embrace the possibility of changing aspects of myself?
- Can I see how starting with self-love would be more conducive to healing?

The psychologist who clung to her MS

The patient with Multiple Sclerosis (MS) consciously chose to maintain her MS symptoms, keeping her husband beholden to the relationship, and avoiding unwanted responsibilities. Therefore, in treatment, it became clear that the "solution" had to address the "problem." If the diagnosis (of MS) was not seen as the problem then how on earth could a solution for the diagnosis be of any help? She refused treatment for her MS. But could she have been helped further if she looked beyond the MS?

Sometimes your vocation (e.g., being a psychologist) can lead to conclusions about your life that shortchange you. She did not realize that a deeper healing would not only address her MS, but also her unhealthy dependence on her husband's guilt-ridden loyalty. True healing is a complete journey and, especially when therapy addresses the whole person, it is impossible to heal a part without healing the whole. Getting rid of MS is not about getting rid of the symptoms of MS; it is about getting rid of the emotional and contributing factors that originally enabled the disease. It is about going beyond your symptoms. It's necessary to know what pre-existed in the relational dynamic, in the first place, which led her to such desperate measures to maintain the relationship at the cost of her own well-being.

The body heals in the reverse order of the apparition of symptoms. In this patient's case, the MS symptoms were the last to appear in her life's time-line and thus the first to disappear. Had she been willing to complete the process, the next symptom would have been her sense of desperation. It too has its roots. In fact those roots preceded her marriage. The desperation was based on the fear of abandonment and the compensatory behaviour she witnessed in her mother. This fear had a factual basis as her father was a top commander in the army and was often away on duty. Her mother lived in fear of losing him, so, when he returned, she tolerated unacceptable behaviours from him in order not to "lose" him emotionally as well.

An established role model spurred conscious and unconscious behaviours in this patient. Her choice to keep her illness had an internal story, something like, "I will teach him, he will look after me now." This was partly payback for her mother's acquiescence to her father and partly motivated by her own unconscious "willingness" to model her mother's role as a victim.

Homeopathy heals in the exact order necessary for inner struggles to be addressed. There is no escaping this process, as one can with psychology. Neither homeopathy nor psychology, though, gives patients all the necessary tools to make sense of their own stories. That process can be guided, but ultimately comes from Self Inquiry as we covered above.

Here are some questions that might have helped this patient if she were open:

- Is it true that my husband will abandon me if I get healthier?
- If my husband leaves me, does this mean I am being abandoned?
- Is it his fault that I have an abandonment issue?
- Does he have problems confronting issues in our relationship?
- Do I have problems confronting my own feelings?
- Do I have problems confronting feelings that come up for him?
- Do I recognize that I am carrying an old story, which is affecting my life?
- What is actually taking place in this relationship?
- What would happen if I understood my own story and were willing to drop it?

In this particular patient, what needed to be addressed was her unhealthy attitude in her relationship. The Multiple Sclerosis was the end result. To heal, she would have needed to be willing to address the initial cause of her dis-balance.

S in in the LISTEN Principles stands for Symptoms and it is very important to take a complete and all-inclusive perspective of what we include as symptoms. I believe health is freedom from physical, mental, emotional, and spiritual constraints. In this context the physical symptoms were just a small part of the whole. It was important to go beyond the symptoms.

As we have covered in the body of the book, there is no separating emotion from its manifestations in our bodies. So when you are gathering your symptoms, a good place to start is with your attitude, temperament, and observing what you are sensitive to: what gets you upset, sad, or frustrated. Don't forget that symptoms represent a dis-balance mentally, emotionally and spiritually. Try to check in on how you are feeling and what experiences come up for you with these feelings. How are you dealing with these emotions and what thoughts do you have surrounding them?

Rate your emotional Pain level:

- How are you dealing with your emotions?
- Do you believe you are suppressing your emotions?
- If so, what does that mean to you?
- Do you believe any of your symptoms are manifestations of your emotions?
- Can you trace back your experience of that particular emotion to its origins?
- What was happening in your life at that time?
- Is the current situation "worth" the symptoms of your emotional investment?
- What is your emotional pain level from 0-10?

Let me give you an example from the psychologist with MS. When she experienced fear of abandonment as a child, it was emotionally charged and seemed real. When she felt that fear as an adult, though, the trigger was less obvious. Yet the emotion was just as strong, if not stronger.

I explain this experience with the analogy of tracks. The first time you experience a strong emotion, it lays tracks. At a future date, when you re-experience this emotion, the tracks are already laid and it takes less to get into the groove and retrigger the emotion. When you are not conscious of this phenomenon you react more intensely to future triggers of this original emotion than the situation warrants.

This pattern creates physiological stress in your body. We are accustomed to understanding stress as an acute short-term event that passes, but many people experience chronic stress which eventually manifests as chronic diseases and that can exacerbate emotional and physical pain.

Chronic pain itself creates long-term physiological stress, which builds up in your body and needs to be addressed. We have elaborated on this in Reboot Your Body.

Are you at risk of impacting your health from long-term stress or pain?

Rate your Stress level?

- On of a scale 0-10, what level of stress are you conscious of experiencing?

- Is there anything in your health that might indicate you have been exposed to long-term stress?
- Do you suffer from high blood pressure?
- Memory loss?
- Unexplained weight gain?

Rate your physical pain level?

- What is the degree of your pain on a scale of 0-10?
- What do you feel about your pain?
- On a scale of 0-10, how intensely are you suffering on account of it?
- What thoughts do you have regarding your level of pain?
- What do you tend to say when talking to others about your pain?
- Do you believe this pain is permanent?
- Are you avoiding activity on account of the pain?
- Have you associated bodily pain with a traumatic event?

As I covered earlier in the book, BowenFirst™ is an ideal way of addressing stress and pain of all kinds. T in LISTEN stands for Touch. It is important to understand that we live in a physical body and despite all our thoughts and feelings, our body has its own capacity to reach homeostasis. Touch is an essential part of healing.

Touch is the trigger to unleashing what the body holds, which holds the 90% percent of your mind that is unconscious.

Associating the symptom in the body with the emotional memory is a way of acknowledging the emotion. Making explicit the mind-body connection plays an integral role in the ability to release the traumatic events stored in the tissues of our body. This enhances healing. Our thoughts can help us visualize and understand what our body is experiencing and serve to interpret what it needs to heal.

One of the most effective ways of regaining your health is attributing "meaning" to your symptoms. This cannot be done purely intellectually. There is an elaborate process to help create the space in which understanding these "meanings" will arise. This process is important: implicit in the self-diagnosis is the solution.

It has been my experience that patients by and large know what their problem is, how they got there, and, when given different options, know what course of treatment will most likely help them.

As we saw prior in the "Plan" chapter of the book, research points to the efficacy of direct patient involvement in the process of healing, established through the patient's own interpretation of the meaning of their symptoms, as well as a clear visual formulation of their intention to potentiate a healing action. A methodology is needed that allows the patient to elaborate on his or her personal meanings of events and the possibilities of alternative meanings. The most important step you can make is to engage in your health.

- Learn what else you can do to support your body's healing process.

- Understand how you are taking responsibility for your health.
- Discover why and how blame and guilt make your body sick
- Learn to be your own health advocate
- Set yourself free.
- So what is your next step?

Do you have a clear intention, commitment and set of goals for starting your healing journey? Do you understand the steps down your own path of healing?

Are you clear on how to transform information and insight into intuition you can trust?

In my LISTEN Principles, I elaborate on the key elements that have helped me and my patients reclaim their health. Might this be the next step for you?

To conclude, I want you to define what health means to you and to remind you of the World Health Organization's definition of health. I am not espousing a policy here, just sharing a definition.

The World Health Organization (WHO) defines health as "*A state of complete physical, mental and social well-being and not merely the absence of disease or infirmity.*"

What is your definition of health? And why?

- Is "symptom free" sufficient?
- What is your relationship to your symptoms?
- Do you see your symptoms as the enemy?
- Do you attribute meaning to your symptoms?

- Are your symptoms helping you address core issues in your life?
- Are you going beyond your symptoms?

What does well-being feel like? Does it allow you to fulfill your life purpose? Enjoy your life better? Do you have dreams? Do you have a vision? Health is the stepping-stone of well being which is an expansive, abundant and free state of being.

It is only when we have done work on ourselves and taken responsibility for our own health, that we can truly understand why health matters, the role health plays in our everyday life and decisions, and its implications for ourselves, our family and loved ones as well as our environment. Through individual health choices, we become greater participants in society and can take appropriate measures with regard to our resources, quality of life and the future of our planet. Join me in this movement.

A Healer in Every Household!

Conclusion

"The science of medicine must be deployed to elucidate the art of medicine; otherwise, medicine falls short, both as science and art."
Miller & Colloca, 2011

In our journey as health care practitioners, doctors and healers, we are challenged with regard to our purpose, not because we did not want to help people, or because we didn't believe that the science and practices of the day had something to offer, but because we actually met our match — our patient.

Those of us who are drawn to read this book realize that our patients are our teachers, and we need to collaborate. Science has given us tools and is today guiding our way to the inevitable conclusion that nothing is whole without all of its parts. There is no science without a subject, and there is no subject without a culture, paradigm and belief system. We can offer little without understanding the context of the whole, and we help only insofar as we resonate with the ideas and ideals of our patients.

Despite our schooling, education and ability to perform varied skill sets — defined as what we do — it is how we do things and why we do them that touches us most. When we come home, we want to share the pleasure it was to help someone, or how openly we shared options with them, or how great and empowered they felt when they left the office.

It is always the human element, the part that has individual meaning that means anything at all. And for the patient, that makes all the difference. It is clear that the mind and heart are the guides of our greater potential to serve.

No one will argue with Harv Eker, author of the Secrets of the Millionaire Mind (2005), that successful entrepreneurs have a clear vision of their goals, and a daily practice to which they are accountable to achieve this goal. They prioritize their time and concentrate on the elements aligned to their vision. The entire business community applauds this approach and young entrepreneurs pay gurus of this vision thousands of dollars to be inspired to carve their own path to success.

But it need not be any different in the field of health care. We have the same mind; We need to step up as Leaders in shifting the focus from disease management to health care. Shift the focus from Prescription to Prevention. As doctors, we are by and large all "Lone Rangers" disconnected from our patients' experiences, in denial of our own, and limited by methods and technologies that are hardly inspirational, motivating and successful.

I am generalizing, but are we not subjected to the same pharmaceutical pressures and to the same "magic pill" society, as is everyone else?

Until the time we can serve as an inspiration and coach to the patient who really wants to take back their health, and wants to be fully responsible for the consequences of all his/her decisions, we will continue to practice "medicine" in a void, bereft of the key elements that really make the difference between "sick" and "healthy."

As I hope I have convinced you, the SOAP form

is fraught with the assumptions that lie at the base of conventional medicine. In fact, it has spawned a "relationship" between the doctor and the patient that is neither conducive to the restoration of health as research has shown, nor aligned with the factors at play in healing.

The patient's "subjective" view of her/his symptoms, which in fact is formed by their understanding of and attributing meaning to the situation, is the prime motivator in improving and reconstructing their health. It is this subjective rendition wherein lies the power to create a new reality, and the possibility of establishing, through their own interpretation of the meaning of their symptomatology, a "prescription" for a change in their health.

The "objective" symptoms and findings are of minimal value when it comes to therapeutic outcomes. It is not the name of the "disease" that decides how it will be manifested or treated in a particular patient. It is decided by the patient and propelled by their alignment with the elements that favour internal healing.

The "assessment" is based on what we perceive is happening, which is informed by our theoretical frame of reference. There is nothing particularly scientific or revealing to come to a "disease" conclusion based on a set of symptoms that are typically associated with it. Nor is it much more of a stretch to "prescribe" the marketed solution for the "disease." What is challenging, and far more rewarding, is to engage the patient in this process and become an agent in their healing journey.

The "plan" is thus the journey, a "road trip" leading to the destination. It is the doctor-patient relationship that is built of congruence of perception, aim and method — a key to aligning for success. In the research of M.J. Simmonds (2000), when discussing placebo, she states:

"The congruence between the patient's and practitioners' beliefs about problems and treatments will potentially affect the patients' efforts, enthusiasm and adherence to treatment, thereby further complicating efforts to distinguish between specific and placebo effects." (Simmonds, 2000)

If congruence can have such a big impact in expected results, let's work with that, regardless of whether it is a result of our therapies or the placebo effect.

Congruence is a GOOD problem to have!

This same author further emphasizes the importance of the context of healing and states, "...benefits of symptomatic treatments are due not to the treatment interventions themselves but to the contexts in which the treatments are delivered." (Simmonds, 2000)

We are talking about congruence and context, both heavily reliant on the doctor — patient relationship. Furthermore, expectation is a primary factor that has shown to affect results, "Scientific assessment of benefits from symptomatic treatments, such as analgesic agents, has been based on the assumption that treatment interventions will produce predictable benefits in patients with a given condition that can be measured in aggregate statistics derived from randomized clinical trials and extrapolated to clinical practice.

"However, placebo and nocebo research reveals that the context in which symptomatic treatments are provided, and notably the information communicated to patients, creates expectations that influence the observed outcomes in terms of which benefits and risks are defined." (Miller & Brody, 2011)

So in establishing our plan, we learn to take into account congruence, context, and expectation. These are all factors established in relationship and cannot be "objectively" measured. And further, we realize that it is not what we do that matters, it is the benefits that patients get as a result of what we do that counts.

From the perspective of the patient in pain, for example, it is unlikely to matter whether pain relief derives entirely, primarily, or not at all from the inherent or characteristic properties of the treatment. The treatment is beneficial insofar as the intervention plus the context in which it is delivered produces benefit to the patient.

In fact, the subjectivity of the patient cannot be taken out of the equation.

"The reputation of modern medicine has been based on its scientific objectivity. Therapeutic power derives from the ability of physicians to discern the facts about disease and its modification by means of treatment interventions. The benefits and risks of therapies are generally understood as deriving entirely from the outcomes of applying the properties of treatment interventions to the objective bodily processes of the patient.

"However, viewing the benefits and risks of symptomatic treatments through the lens of the placebo and nocebo phenomena reveals that therapeutic benefits and risks of harm from these treatments cannot be determined independently of the subjectivity of the patient. The placebo and nocebo principles are not brute facts about pathophysiology and its modification by medical technology." (Miller & Brody, 2011,pp 229-243)

In other words, it is often the commitment and alignment to what one feels is right that makes the difference, not the actual procedure, treatment or medication taken as they are by necessity part and parcel of the context.

As we have seen, there is an increased therapeutic effect if the patient is aligned with the treatment and has positive reinforcement of the outcomes. Research also supports the notion that the patient's increased control over their health and body has beneficial effects. Approaches to treatment that encourage patient empowerment and that share tools for better control of reactions to stress, act to favorably reinforce the direction of patients' health outcomes and are essential to consider in the treatment "Plan."

We have furthermore established that from the perspective of the patient the "mind-body" connection exists not only in a theoretical way but has clear biological pathways. We have also raised the point that despite these pathways, there are individual variations due to the individual's "coping" skills. These skills may be in part related to personality traits as well as to a past traumatic memory that activates and sensitizes these pathways.

We have also shown that pain perception is directly influenced by suggestions both positive and negative. So how can it be that we value the "scientific double blind studies" that are limited by their context and subject to individual variances, to the detriment of the doctor -patient relationship?

In conclusion, it seems evident to me that the practice

of medicine is more an Art than a Science. Now science has finally backed the art that must be involved.

The time is so ripe to step up to the challenge of putting all our differences aside and working on the larger issues at hand. Can health be achieved with the current environmental challenges we are facing: nuclear fall-out, electro-magnetic fields, water and air pollution, food contamination, and unsound monoculture farming methods?

Is health all about adaptation, and is our goal to help people adapt? Is it about finding peace of mind in the midst of all this cause and effect turmoil, and defining our personal balance? These are the real questions.

Ultimately, the doctor-patient relationship is a relationship in that context. Like all relationships, the more congruent, supportive, inspiring and positively challenging it is, the healthier it is.

Imagine the huge shift in our health care if all of us questioned the current medical "beliefs" and explored how we could regain our autonomy. We should never lose sight of our souls' journey, and the reason we were drawn to this field in the first place.

Sometimes the solutions are easier than the problems we believe we must solve. We have full control over what we choose to put in our bodies and over what thoughts we put into our minds. It is time we take a stand for health. Take personal responsibility. Find a collaborative health team that is not swayed by economically based agendas and Reboot our World!

Author Biography

 Dr. Manon Bolliger promotes patient consciousness in the healing process. Over the past two decades, Dr. Bolliger has treated thousands of patients and taught thousands of professional medical health care providers. Beyond trauma and pain relief, her diversified experience guides individuals through a healing process, which is both empowering and nurturing, highlighting the importance of truly "listening" to your body with compassion and love.

Dr. Bolliger is well positioned to portray both sides of this patient-doctor journey, having personal experiences with scoliosis, Cancer and Multiple Sclerosis.

Throughout her personal and academic journey, Manon is lead by her desire to understand what makes people change, grow, heal, and celebrate life. Dr. Bolliger currently lives on Bowen Island, BC. having established a successful following from her earlier practice in rural Nova Scotia and Ontario.

While overcoming stage 4 CA without pharmaceutical or a hysterectomy, she discovered that we are accustomed to thinking that conflict resolution is mediated externally. But when it comes to health, it is an internal process. She has pioneered the 'A Healer in Every Household' Movement embracing the body's capacity to heal and the choice to govern our lives.

She has spoken on international stages like JTFoxx's Money, Health, and Business, has an upcoming TEDx talk in

Las Vegas, is the host of The Healer's Cafe podcast and has appeared on ABC, CTV and NBC.

www.facebook.com/DrManonBolliger
twitter.com/DrManonBolliger
www.youtube.com/user/DrManonBolliger
www.linkedin.com/in/DrManonBolliger

Citations

Alder R, C. N. (1990). Annual Review of Pharmacology and Toxicology.

Alder R, C. N. (1981). Psychoneuroimmunology.

Anderson Robert M, F. M. (2010). Patient Empowerment/Pa 1 tient Education and Counseling.

Andrews, Paul w. et.al. (2011) Blue again: perturbational effects of antidepressants suggest monoaminergic homeostasis in major depression

Andrews, Paul, Frontiers in Evolutionary Psychology.2011

Antoinette IN, L. V.-S. (2011). Induction of Nocebo and Placebo Effects on Itch and Pain by Verbal Suggestion.

Apkarian. (2008). Progress in Neurobiology

Arntz, A. a. (2004). The Meaning of Pain Influences Its Experienced Intensity.

Arthritis Care and Research. (2001).

Atherton, K, et al(2006): Predictors of persistent neck pain after whiplash injury Emerg Med J. March;
doi: 10.1136/emj.2005.027102

Geraldine Aubert , Peter M. Lansdorp
Physiological ReviewsPublished 1 April 2008Vol. 88no. 557-579

Azar, Beth, 2001,Vol32, No.11 A new take on psychoneuroimmunology

B.A. (2001). A New Take on Psychoneuroimmunology. American Psychological Association.

Bannister, D. a. (1986). Inquiring Man: The psychology of Personal Constructs (3 ed.). Croom Helm, London.

Barnsley L, Lord S, Bogduk N. Clinical Review, Whiplash injury. Pain 1994

Benedetti F, L. M. (2007). When Words are Painful.

Benedetti F, P. A. (2003). Conscious Expectations and Unconscious Conditioning in Analgesic, Motor and Hormonal Placebo/Nocebo Responses.

Benson, H. (1975). The Relaxation Response. Harper Collins.

Bernard B. Lanter, Karin Sauer and David G. Davies. Bacteria Present in Carotid Arterial Plaques Are Found as Biofilm Deposits Which May Contribute to Enhanced Risk of Plaque Rupture. mBio, June 2014 DOI: 10.1128/mBio.01206-14

Blauer-Wu, s. (2002). Psychoneuroimmunology Part 1: Physiology. Clinical. Journal of Oncology Nursing

Bloom FE, L. A. (2000). Brain, Mind and Behavior (3 ed.). Worth, New York.

Bosma, FK, Kessels RPC, Cognitive Impairments, Psychological Dysfunction, and Coping Styles in Patients With Chronic Whiplash Syndrome, Neuropsychiatry, Neuropsychology Behav Neurol 2002 Brodie EE, W. A. (2007). Analgesia Through The Looking Glass A randomized controlled trial investigating the effect of viewing a 'virtual' limb upon phantom limb pain, sensation and movement. Eur J Pain?

Brydon L, Walker C, Wawrzyniak A, Whitehead D, Okamura H, Yajima J, Tsuda A, Steptoe A. (2009). Synergistic effects of psychological and immune stressors on inflammatory cytokine and sickness responses in humans. Brain Behav Immun.. PMID 18835437 doi:10.1016/j.bbi.2008.09.007

Buchbinder R, O. R. (2009). New England Journal of Medicine.

Byron, K. Loving What Is.

Cannon, W. (1915). Bodily Changes in Pain, Hunger, Fear and Rage. D. Appleton and Co., New York.

Carver, C.S. & Scheier, M.F. (1982) Control theory: A useful conceptual framework for personality_social, Clinical and health psychology. Psychological Bulletin.

Carver, C.S., & Scheier, M.F. (1998). On the self-regulation of behaviour. New Yrk: Cambridge University Press.

Cedraschi C, N. M. (1998). Baillieres Clin Rheumatol.

Cedraschi C, R. J. (1999). Definations of a Problem and Prolembs of a Definiation.

Chapman et al., 1959

Chordas, T. (1996). Embodiment and Experience. Cambridge University Press.

Chrousos, G. P. & Gold, P. W. The concepts of stress and stress system disorders: overview of physical and behavioral homeostasis. JAMA 267, (1992).

Cohen, Milton, Department of Rheumatology, in New South Wales, Australia. Pain Medicine and Its Models: Helping or Hindering? Volume 9, Issue 7, October 2008

Colloca L, B. F. (2005). Placebos and painkillers: Is mind as real as matter? Nature
Reviews Neuroscience

Colloca L, L. L. (2004). Overt Versus Covert Treatment for Pain, Anxiety and Parkinson's Disease. Lancet Neurology

Colloca L, S. M. (2008). The Role of Learning in Nocebo and Placebo Effects.

Coats, T.L. Brenstein, D.G., Nangia, N.K., Brown, M.T., 2004. Effects of valdecoxib in the treatment of chronic low back pain: results of a randomized, placebo-controlled trial. Clin. Ther.

Cosgrove L, Bursztajn HJ, Kupfer DJ, Regier DA. "Toward Credible Conflict of Interest Policies in Clinical Psychiatry" Psychiatric Times 26:1.

Crane, L. The Release Technigque.

D.S. K. (1997). Brain Longevity. Warner Books.

Diers, M. (2010). A Fascinating Study in Pain.

Diers, M. (2010). Pain.

Dr., A. D. (2010). Change Your Brain, Change Your Body. Harmony Books.

Dunn KM, C. P. (2006). Repeat Assessment Improves the Prediction of Prognosis in Patients with Low-Back Pain in Primary Care.

Dunn KM, J. K. (2006). Am J Epidemiol.

Dunn KN, C. P. (2006). The Importance of Symptom Duration in Determining Prognosis.

Dunn, K. M. (2008). Pain.

Dworkin, R. H. (2010). Pain.

E.M. (1999). Europen Journal of Pain.

Edgar, D. (2011). "Prevention of neural hypersensitivity after acute upper limb burns: Development and pilot of a cortical training protocol" in Science Direct. 2011 Elsevier Ltd and ISBI. Burns 37 Burns. Elsevier Ltd. and ISBI.

Eker, H. (2005). Secrets of the Millionaire Mind. Harper Collins.

Ehrlich, G.E., 2003.Low back pain. Bull. World Health Organ

Engel, G. (1977). The need for a new medical model: A challenge for biomedicine. Science.

Ernst, E. (2001). The Desktop Guide to Complimentary and Alternative Medicine. (L. Mosby, Ed.)

Ferrari, R, Russell, AS, Best Pract Res Clin Rheumatol, 2003 Feb;17

Flaten MA, A. P. (2006). Cognitive and Emotional Factors in Placebo Analgesia.

Flaten MA, S. T. (1999). Drug Related Information Generates Placebo and Nocebo Responses That Modify the Drug Response.

Freeman L, L. G. (2001). Mosby's Complimentary & Alternative Medicine: A Research Approach. Mosby, St. Louis MO.

Friston, K. (2011). Bid Cyborn.

Friston, K. (2011). Biol Cybern.

Furase, K. (2007). Neuroscience Letters.

G, M. F. (2011). Theor Med Bioeth.

Garrdo, M. I. (2009). Clinical neurophysiology.

Garrido, M. L. (2009). Neurolmage.

GB, A. (1999). Epidemiological Features of Lowe Back Pain. Lancet.

Glenmullen, Joseph,M.D., (2000) Prozac Backlash, (Simon & Schuster, New York),

Goffaux P, d. S. (2009). Pain Relief Through Expectation Supercedes Descending Inhibitory Deficits in Fibromyalgia Patients.
Guez, M. Chronic Neck Pain. Ume8 University, Sweden.

Guez. M., et.al. Chronic neck pain of traumatic and non-traumatic origin. A population based study. Acta Orthop Scand 2003;

Guyton, A.,& Hall,J. (2006). Textbook of medical physiology, 11th edition. Philadelphia: W.B. Saunders

Hahnemann, S. Organaon of the Medical Art (6 ed.). (B. O. Washington, Ed.)

Haugli, L. a. (2000). Patient Education and Counseling. Volume 41, Issue 2 , September 2000

Haugli, L. a. (2001). Patient Education and Counseling.

Haugli, L. (2001). Patient Education & Councelling.

Haugli, L. The Body Has a History.

Hendriks E J, Scholten Peeters G G, van der Windt D A. et al Prognostic factors for poor recovery in acute whiplash patients. Pain 2005. 114408–416.416. [PubMed]

Herbert TB, C. S. (1993). Psychosom Med.

Hetu, S. (2010). Neuroscience.

How Your Brain Reacts to Stress. (2011). The Franklin Institure On-Line.

Horgan, John, Psychiatry in Crisis! Mental Health Director Rejects Psychiatric "Bible" and Replaces with....Nothing. May 4,2013 http://blogs.scientificamerican.com/WSS/post.php?blog=45&post=1173

I ASP, "Part III: Pain Terms, A Current List with Definitions and Notes on Usage" (pp 209-214) Classification of Chronic Pain, Second Edition, IASP Task Force on Taxonomy, edited by H. Merskey and N. Bogduk, IASP Press, Seattle, ©1994.

I, T. (2010). Nature Medicine.

I., K. (1999). How Expectancies Shape Experience. American Psychological Association, Washington DC.
J, M. (2000). Journal Title, 287 (5451).
J, S. M. (2000). Pysiotherapy (Vol. 86).

J acobs, G.D. (2001). The physiology of mind-body interactions: The stress response and the Relaxation Response. The Journal of Alternative and Complementary Medicine

Jensen JP, K. P. (2001). Handbook of Pain Assessment. (M. R. Turk DC, Ed.) Guilford Press, New York.

Johnston, G.R., Webster, N.R. (2009) Cytokines and the immunomodulatory function of the vagus nerve, British Journal of Anaesthesia (2009) doi:10.1093/bja/aep037

K allmes DF, C. B. (2009). New England Journal of Medicine.

Kelly, G. (1955). The psychology of Personal Constructs. Norton, New York.

Khalsa, Singh, 1997, Brain Longevity. Warner Books

Kilner, J. M. European Journal of Neuroscience (Vol. 32). 2010.

Kilner, J. M. (2007). Predictive-Coding: An Account of the Mirror Neuron System.

Kilner, J. M. (2007). Review Gognitive Process.

Klazen CAH, L. P. (2010). Vertos II.

L aarhoven, et. al, in 2011
laleva.org/eng/2004/05/louis_pasteur_vs_antoine_bchamp_and_ the_germ_theory_of_disease_causation_2.html

Lakoff, G. a. (1981). Metaphores We Live By. The University of Chicgo Press Chicago.

Lepore, S.J., Miles, H.J., & Levy,J.S. (1997) Relation of chronic and episodic stressors to psychological distress, reactivity, and health problems. International Journal of Behavioural Medicine

Levenson, L. The Sedona Method.

Loeser, J. (1982). Concepts of Pain. (B. R. Stanton -Hicks J, Ed.) Raven Press, New York.

M , L. M. (2006). Alternative Journal of Nursing (Vol. 11).

M, V. K. (1994). Studying the Natural History of Back Pain, Spine.

Maler SF, W. E. (1993). Brain Res. PubMed

Mate, G. (2004). When the Body Says No. Random House.

McGorry RW, W. B. (2000). The Relation Between Pain Intensity, Disability and the Episodic Nature of Chronic and Recurrent Low Back Pain, Spine.

Melzach R. Pain measurement and Assessment New York: Raven Press, 1983

Merleau-Ponty, M. (1996). Phenomenology of Perception (Vol. 10). Routledge & Kegan .

Merleau-Ponty, M. (1996). Phenomenology of Perceptions (10 ed.). Routledge & Kegan London.

Miller FG, B. H. (2011). Understanding and Harnessing Placebo Effects.

Miller Franklin G, C. L. (2011). The Placebo Phenomenonand Medical Ethics. O. Spring Science and Business Media.

Miller, F. G. (2011). The Placebo Phenomenon and Medical Ethics. Springer Science & Business.

Miller, F. G. (2001). Theor Med Bioeth (wo11).

Montgomery GH, K. I. (1997). Classical Conditioning and the Placebo Effect.

Nauert, Rick, Phd, 2011 Antidepressants May Up Risk of Relapse. http://psychcentral.com/news/2011/07/20/antidepressants-may-up-risk-of-relapse/27903.html

National University of Singapore, Psychosom Med 2014 July 4. The Use of Neuroimaging to Advance the Understanding of Chronic Pain: From Description to Mechanism. Derbyshire SW.

Neale Michael C, G. et. al. (2011). : Perturbational Effects of Antidepressants Suggest Monoaminergic Homeostasis in Major Depression.FrontiersinPsychology.2DOI:10.3389/fpsyg.2011.00159

Neimeyer, R. a. (1995). Constructivist psychotherapies (American Psychological Association, Washington ed.)

Nestler, Winter 2008 Issue: Volume 3 Number 1 www.nlm.nih.gov/medlineplus/magazine/issues/.../winter08.html

Nygard, R. (1993). Agent or Pawn. ad Notam Gylendal.

Olesen J, G. P. (2003). The International Classification of Headache Disorders (2 ed.). Lancet Neurol.

Oshman, James, (2003), Energy Medicine in Therapeutics and Human Performance.

Pelletier, K. (2002). Mind as Healer, Mind as Slayer: Mind Body Medicine Comes of Age.

Pert CB, R. M. (1985). J Immunol, Aug 135 (2 suppl).

Pike, A. J. (2008). Physical Therapy Reiviews (Vol. 13).

Pike, A. J. (2008). Physical Therapy Reviews (Vol. 13).

Pope, M. a. (1981). Personal Consturct Psychology and Education. Academic Press, London.

Post-White, J. &. (2002). Complimentary/Alternative theories in Nursing (4 ed.). (M. S. Lindquist, Ed.)

Price DD, M. L. (1999). An Analysis of Factors That Contribute to the Magnitude of Placebo analgesia in an Experimetal Design.

Pringle, Evelyn,(2006) "TeenScreen—Normal Kids Labeled Mentally Ill," Scoop Independent News, 2 Aug.

Purves, D et. al. (2004) Neuroscience Third Edition

Quinlan, J. Psychoneuroimmunology - Can We Control Our Immune Systems?

Ramachandran VS, R.-R. D. (1996). Synesthesia In Phantom Limbs Induced with Mirrors. Pro R Soc Lond B Biol Sci.

Raspe H, H. A. (2003). Theeories and Models of Chronicity. Schmerz.

Robertson Maggie, M. J. (2011). A Discourse Analysis of Decision Sharing in General Practice.

Ruff M, S. E. (1985). Clin Immunol Immunopathal Dec., 37.

S. L. J. (1999). Medical Care and Review (2 ed., Vol. 56).
Sauer, S. (2010). Self regulation as a framework for understanding and treating chronic pain disorders. S.E. Sauer et al. in Clinical Psychology Review 2010; .E.Sauer et al)

Schafer A., T. N. (2000). Manual Therapy.

Schmidt,J., & Carlson,C.R. (2009) A controlled comparison of emotional reactivity and physiological response in masticatory muscle pain Patients. Journal of Orofacial Pain Services, D. o. (2006). Functional Links Between the Immune System, Brain Function and Behavior.

Sheather-Reid, R. B. , Cohen, Milton,Journal of Pain & Symptom Management (Vol. 15 No. 4 April 1998)

Simmonds, M. (2000). Pain and the Placebo in Physiotherapy. A Benevolent lie? Physiotherapy

Smith K. (2002). Complimentary/Alternative Theories in Nursing (4 ed.). (M. S. Lindquist, Ed.) Springer, New York.

Spiegel, D. (2008). NIH Medline Plus (Vol. 3).

Staats P, H. H. (1998). Suggestion/Placebo Effects on Pain.

Steen H, H. L. (2001). Patient Education and Counseling .

Streather-Reid, R. B. (1998). Effacy of Analgesics in Chronic Pain. Elsevier, New York.

T aranka, M. (2011). Brain Research (Vol. 1412).

Thornton, J. (1993). The Sugar Pill Secret.

Tanaka, M. (2011). Central inhibition regulates motor output during physical fatigue" (Brain Research 1412v(2011) Tanaka, M et. Al.,) Brain Research (Vol. 1412).

Tick, Heather,MD Holistic Pain Releief; New World Library, 2013.

Tracey, I. 2010. Getting the pain you expect: Mechanisms of placebo, nocebo and reappraisal effects
in humans. Nature Medicine 16

Travell J. and Simons D., Myofascial pain and dysfunction; The Trigger Point Manuel, 2 vols. (batimore:Williams and Wilkins,1992)

Turk DC, M. R. (2001). Handbook of Pain Assessment. (M. R. Turk DC, Ed.) Guilford Press, New York.

Turk DC, et al (2002) Psychological Factors in Chronic Pain: Evolution and Revolution; Journal of Consulting and Clinical Psychology. Vol. 70, No. 3

Turk DC, R. T. (1988). Toward an Empirically Derived Taxonomy of Cronic Pain Patients. (J. C. Psychol, Ed.)

Tuzun, E. H. (2007). Quality of Life in Chronic Musculoskeletal Pain (Vol. 21).

Van Larhoven AIM, K. F.-S. (2010). Hererotopic Pruritic Conditioning and Itch - Analogous to DNIC in Pan?

Von Korf M, M. D. (2005). A Prognostic Approach to Defining Chronic Pain.

Von Korff M, M. D. (2006). Proceedings of the 11th World Congress on Pain of the International Association for the Study of Pain. (F. H, Ed.) IASP Press.

Von Korff, M. (2008). Chronic pain Reconsidered.

Take back control of your own health! How do I find out more?

Follow the link and help yourself to the free videos and dowloads offered at
www.DrManonBolliger.com

Subscribe to my podcast- The Healer's Cafe
www.drmanonbolliger.com/the-healers-cafe-podcast/

Sign up for:
www.rebootyourbody.info for a free webinar and to learn more how to address stress and keep your body functioning optimally.

Follow me on:
www.facebook.com/DrManonBolliger
twitter.com/DrManonBolliger
www.youtube.com/user/DrManonBolliger
www.linkedin.com/in/DrManonBolliger

If you are a health practitioner, feel free to contact us at www.bowencollege.com

www.facebook.com/TheBowenCollege
www.twitter.com/BowenCollege
www.youtube.com/user/TheBowenCollege/featured
www.linkedin.com/in/DrManonBolliger

"The Reason Why?

"Each day, all around us, is chatter, whether it comes from within or life in general. We constantly receive, hear and see so much; we are now so socially conditioned we are immune to what our bodies are saying, and yes, they do speak. In fact, there is usually a plethora of reasons why we can't, won't or don't want to hear the message. Our bodies speak in in many ways, and once we lose control it speaks to us with pain, hurt, or anguish regardless of whether the origin of our distress is mental, physical or spiritual.

How delightful it is to discover the highly evolved and competent team of expert therapist and associates of Doctor Manon. Her professional team, is able to clearly hear and interrupt the body's message allowing this unique process of inquiry to cut to the chase and bring to consciousness the core healing issues while using the body as a vehicle; thus allowing the treatment and making the outcome often almost immediate and very effective. Allowing us to take back control and give the body what it needs rather than what we think it needs.

Locating and healing the cause is usually relaxing, always effective, painless, and non-invasive while it continues to improve our overall mind and body health for sometime, afterwards.

Finding the correct diagnosis is indeed the hardest part, not curing the illness. It is our body alone and the symptoms it projects which speak to us, and should we want to listen, it is our body that will tell us what is needed.

Be surprised, we are complex and unique individuals and the outcome maybe vastly different to our perceived interruption of the symptoms!

Dr. Manon's book, 'A Healer In Every Household: Simple Solution for Stress' *brings a wealth of knowledge and understanding to the reader who dares ask the questions. She has her bases covered and shares answers to many questions that those qualified to answer, don't choose to share. With insights into Dr. Manon's own health crises we share her experiences and glimpse her solid unwavering inner strength and how she rallied in her positive beliefs to find the cause and then the cure. Allowing her to become a more informed, knowledgeable and well-balanced individual, not because of, but in spite of, the journey her remarkable life has taken.*

This book brings you many of the answers and understanding you require in your quest to consciously survive and achieve the healthy lifestyle we all desire. Not to read it would be a mistake for our awareness and forward thinking intellect as knowledgeable human beings. With our desire for continued growth into understanding the health and future of our survival this book answers many of the questions and leads us forward with a healthy knowledge to persuade it."

Mary Weizenbach, psychologist